OmStruck

HEALING HEARTBREAK
THROUGH YOGA
AND MEDITATION

AZALEA ART PRESS
Berkeley . California
azaleaartpress@gmail.com
azaleaartpress.blogspot.com
510.919.6117

ISBN 10: 09846977-0-5
ISBN 13: 978-09846977-0-0

Library of Congress
Cataloguing-in-Publication Data
has been applied for.

Cover Photo Credit:
Yolanda Mendoza
YMendoza Photography
510.435.4357
www.YMendozaPhotography.com

**To the broken hearted:
Have faith, there's hope…**

Author's Note:

While the ancient practices of yoga and meditation have proven to be safe and effective, the methods described in this book should be taken as advice only and not as a substitute for medical care. Please seek the treatment of a medical professional if it is deemed necessary.

Acknowledgements:

My deepest gratitude goes to my wonderful, loving family and friends for their love, support, and encouragement.

I would like to thank Tricia De Jesus-Gutierrez, Theresa Harrington, and Megan Banta for reading and editing the manuscript and providing valuable comments and insight.

Yoga instructors Wendy Beckerman, Bruce Guterman and Sarah Pascual deserve my profound respect and appreciation for their generosity and wealth of insight, knowledge and inner wisdom. You have my eternal support.

Wholehearted appreciation must be bestowed on Yolanda Mendoza who captured the light of the morning and the essence of serenity so beautifully in her amazing photographs.

To my publisher, Karen Mireau, for helping me realize my ultimate dream come true and for recognizing the creative, literary spirit that dwells within me.

And for all those who continue to inspire me every day, I honor you with my sincerest praise.

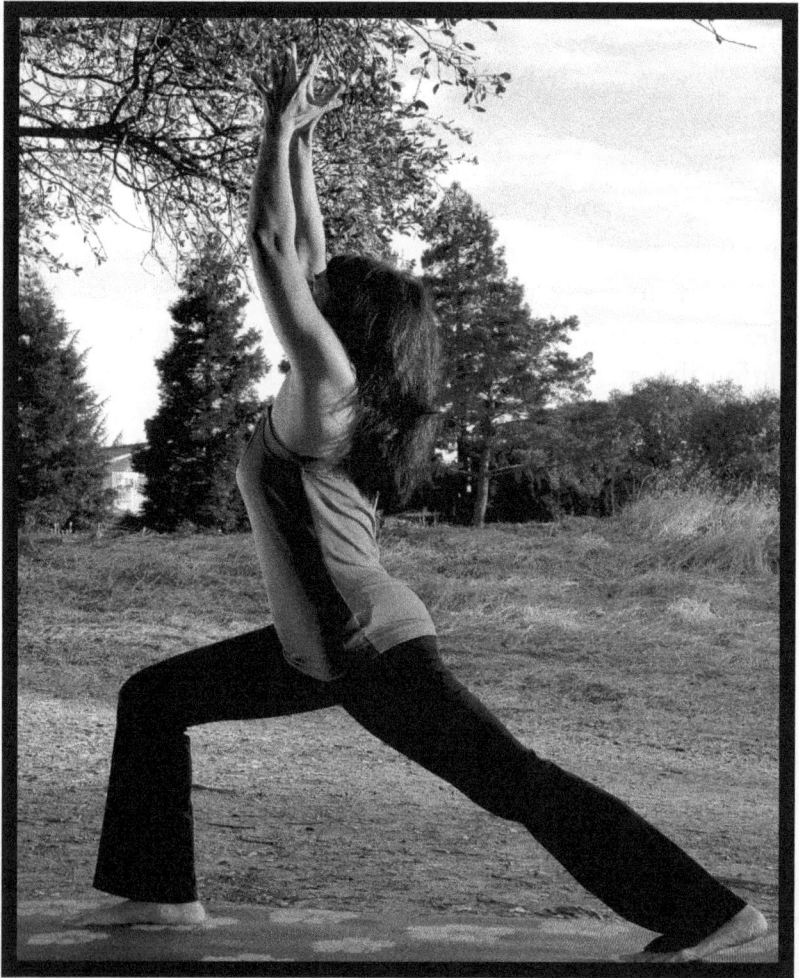

CONTENTS

Introduction   i

Part One:
The Surreal Life:
Facing Your Past
& Putting it Behind You

Chapter 1:
Allow Yourself to Grieve   1

Chapter 2:
Cry to Purify   8

Chapter 3:
Put Your Heart on Paper   10

Chapter 4:
Gratitude   13

Chapter 5:
Tender Loving Care   16

Chapter 6:
Practice Makes (Im)Perfect   21

Chapter 7:
Love Yourself to Heal Yourself   24

Part Two
The Real World:
Anchoring Yourself in the Present

Chapter 8:
You are Going Now-Here   31

Chapter 9:
Minding Your Manners   36

Chapter 10:
Journaling   39

Chapter 11:
Walking (or Running) in Spirit   45

Chapter 12:
The Five 'Ws' of Yoga
& Meditation   48

Chapter 13:
Search & Rescue,
Search & Recovery   54

Chapter 14:
Getting Through Weekend
& Holiday Blues   57

Chapter 15:
Creating Your Own Power Spots   61

Chapter 16:
Warding Off Negative Energy,
Thoughts & Actions   64

Chapter 17:
The Gift of a Furry Friend   **71**

Chapter 18:
Nothing Lasts Forever   **75**

Chapter 19:
Do Unto Others   **78**

<u>Part Three:</u>
<u>Keeping it Real:</u>
<u>Now, the Future & Beyond</u>

Chapter 20:
The Three R's   **85**

Chapter 21:
Beginner's Mind   **88**

Chapter 22:
In Someone Else's Shoes   **91**

Chapter 23:
Compassion & Beyond   **97**

Chapter 24:
Change Your Attitude,
Change Your Life   **102**

Chapter 25:
Smile Though Your Heart
is Breaking: Laughing On
& Off the Mat   **104**

Chapter 26:
What the Yogis Say   107

Chapter 27:
A Yogi's Healing Journey
After Heartbreak   114

Chapter 28:
From Heartbreaking
to Heart-Opening   120

Chapter 29:
Looking Back to Look Forward   125

Chapter 30:
Dipping Your Toes
in the Pool of Life   132

Chapter 31
With Each Breath   137

References   140

Resources   141

Suggested Reading   142

About the Author   147

Some people come into our lives,
leave footprints on our hearts,
and we are never ever the same.

—Eleanor Roosevelt

Introduction

This is as much a book about heartbreak as it is about yoga and meditation.

Today, as I sit in the public library in Hercules, California gazing out the ceiling to floor windows at the cars whizzing by, I think about how life continues on—the world still turns. Meanwhile I seem to be stuck, tediously clawing my way out of the past—the past that still plagues me to this day.

The trauma of my recent breakup has left me emotionally paralyzed. Yet, as I write about heartbreak, not just from the perspective of someone who's experienced it before in previous relationships and survived, but from the place of one who's still going through the grieving process, I do hope to heal someday. This is the wisdom I strive to impart to you.

This is intended as a book you can turn to for guidance, written by someone whose heart was broken before and who survived the pain. Six years ago, a man I was madly in love with rejected me without explanation and was never heard from again. While I didn't turn to yoga and meditation at the time, I thought going to church regularly would pull me through. It didn't. I started reciting positive affirmations which I thought seemed to work, but I didn't say them often enough.

In short, I really didn't dedicate enough time and effort to enriching my spiritual life.

Just when I decided I would take some time to get to know and love myself more, a special man walked into my life. Actually, he danced into my life. We met at a salsa dance class, started out as salsa buddies and then became lovers. Over time, the easygoing nature of the relationship, our common passion for cats and other animals, his vegetarianism and my transitioning into vegetarianism, our ability to find humor in the same things, and our genuine caring for each other evolved into a friendship and what I believed was a nurturing relationship. I gave up my intention to stay single or unattached for a while to find myself and instead, I gave into love.

So in the process of choosing to love a man, I put working on loving myself on hold. During the relationship, I meditated less and barely practiced yoga, preferring instead to devote all my energies to my boyfriend and our relationship.

Let me back up for a bit. I started practicing yoga in 1999 at my former gym where I was introduced to "gym yoga," the type that placed more emphasis on the physical rather than the spiritual aspect of the practice. I continued "gym yoga" off and on for the next four years until the guy I was dating in 2003 broke up with me. I then turned to meditation courtesy of a three-month meditation class at Buddha Gate Monastery in Lafayette, California. Through the classes, I learned about Buddhism and embraced its concepts, especially that of the principle of nonattachment, nonharming and living in the present.

Except for an occasional yoga and meditation class, through the subsequent years, I remained spiritually unfulfilled. I instinctively knew my soul was famished—it was practically reaching out for nourishment. But I chose to focus on the demands of my external world—my career as a newspaper reporter, the writing of my three novels, graduate school, and of course, my relationship with the man I met in salsa dance class.

I believed the source of my spiritual nourishment came from the time my then boyfriend and I fostered litters of kittens from the local animal shelter—a two-year labor of love. The experience of socializing, feeding and loving these kittens and helping them increase their chances of finding good homes was extremely rewarding.

After our last batch of kittens got adopted in early 2009, I felt an enormous sense of loss—a sort of "empty nest syndrome," if you will—but I was looking forward to fostering again in the spring.

That was when I felt a shift that's still hard to explain even as I look back and ponder the source of that change to this day. Collectively, the country seemed to be in a euphoric, hopeful state when Barack Obama was inaugurated. My then boyfriend seemed to be in good spirits as he finally finished construction on his home office which for some time had been a makeshift foster kitten nursery. I had just finished revisions on my two novels and had already sent one manuscript to a publisher and prepared to shop for literary agents to represent me.

What happened in early 2009 was the catalyst for my taking up yoga and meditation again full force. My boyfriend of four-and-a-half years broke up with me and I felt that I not only lost him but myself as well. I knew that to heal and survive, I had to do more than just get over the heartbreak; I needed to discover who I was, what I really wanted in life and truly love and appreciate my authentic self.

Through my heartache, I rediscovered yoga and meditation and embraced spirituality again through my classes at a spiritually oriented yoga studio in Albany, California, located in an eclectic, diverse strip of businesses and homes east of San Francisco.

Now I am reaching out to the broken hearted through what I do best—writing. This book is a testament to my ongoing path toward healing because I know that healing doesn't just end when the hurting finally stops. Healing, rediscovering and loving yourself is a lifelong journey. I invite you to take this journey with me through yoga and meditation.

In retrospect, I know now that I had to have my heart broken in the worst way possible to become whole again. I am blessed to have the support of loving family and friends. Yet, I still long to complete myself and to love myself more fully. Yoga and meditation are my tools for healing and rediscovering my authentic self.

I'm not a psychologist, psychiatrist, nor a psychotherapist—but a woman in love whose heart was shattered. I know all too well that a broken heart is a serious injury—one that damages the spirit. I'm writing in the moment from a place of experience, the same experience which many of you may relate to but may not know how to begin to cope with. You may need some guidance along the path toward healing. But be reassured—you can heal yourself. While I am not a yoga instructor and I have never led a meditation session, I am writing from my experiences as a yoga student and meditation practitioner and intend to share with you what has worked for me so far.

Why am I writing this book now instead of waiting for years from now when I'm finally over my ex? While I am aware other books preach about mending a broken heart or letting go of a loved one, I am specifically writing this as I heal from my own broken heart. I am fully entrenched in the power of the present as I share my journey toward healing with you. As I anchor myself in the here and now, I am confident that one day, with faith and trust in myself and the process of life, I will be healed. I sincerely wish the same for you.

I ask, during this journey, that you be mindful of the fact that pain and suffering, like love, is universal. What is painful to one person may not seem earth shattering to another. Try to approach my pain, as you approach your own and that of others, with genuine compassion.

I hope that you will, from this reading experience, come away with a respect and understanding that everyone hurts and grieves differently and that we shouldn't compare anyone's situation to another's or even to our own. My pain is my own, just as your pain is yours and no one has the right to tell us otherwise.

Ultimately, we should all learn to embrace this painful, but meaningful experience of getting our hearts broken as an opportunity to heal and grow.

Namaste.

Janice De Jesus
August, 2009

Part One

The Surreal Life:
Facing Your Past
& Putting It Behind You

*The only real mistake is the one
from which we learn nothing.*

—John Powell
<u>The Secret of Staying in Love</u>

Chapter 1:
Allow Yourself to Grieve

When my boyfriend announced to me without warning that he was "done with the relationship," I couldn't believe what I'd just heard. It was a surreal moment, suspended in time—I thought I might have misunderstood his words. This couldn't be happening.

Knowing that a perfect relationship was practically nonexistent and that we could always work out whatever needed working out, I didn't think we had the kind of issues that warranted the need for a breakup.

I had no idea at the time that a breakup could be a blessing in disguise for someone who may have wandered from the spiritual path and needed that wake-up call to bring her back on track. All I could think of at the time my boyfriend said we were over was how devastated I was. How could I possibly go on without him?

I sensed that my boyfriend had a friendship with a woman that was beginning to escalate. This woman, whom I never heard him mention until she showed up one day to pick cherries from his cherry tree at his home in May 2008, suddenly reappeared in his life. He said they had been neighbors and friends before he met me; but, if they were such good friends, why hadn't he mentioned her before in the years we'd been together? Granted, we weren't obliged to tell each other everything, but I thought I knew most of his closest friends, some of whom I've had the pleasure of spending time with.

In retrospect, I think my then-boyfriend made an extra effort to show me that this woman and he were just friends when all three of us hung out together. Frankly, I didn't think it was such a big deal back then. I thought she had a pleasant demeanor but I sensed she kept her distance, at least from me.

Their friendship came into question when the woman started calling my boyfriend numerous times and leaving several long-winded messages on his home phone voice mail. I had no doubt she was inundating him with e-mails as well. He didn't seem to mind. But I did. I may have been a bit jealous, but I was more annoyed that she was overstepping her boundaries. What kind of a woman would constantly hound another woman's boyfriend? I certainly have enough sense not to do that. I would never bombard a male friend with my presence and invade his girlfriend's relationship space. That was out of line.

For all her talk about being compassionate and considerate to all living beings, this woman certainly didn't show any compassion toward me. She probably thought her behavior could pass as an innocent exchange between friends, but I knew better. Why couldn't my boyfriend tell her to back off as her actions were making me uncomfortable?

My anxiety over this woman's unfailing presence led me to take a yoga class on Saturday mornings at a nearby community center in Concord. I also followed that up with a half-day meditation retreat at Buddha

Gate Monastery. To supplement my yoga practice, I attended an Iyengar-style yoga class in Pleasant Hill. Still, in February 2009, something was missing—an internal connection with myself. I had yet to embrace my yoga and meditation practice more fully.

On the night I "caught" my then boyfriend and the woman dining alone together at a nearby Indian restaurant (when he said he would be at the brewery with his friends), how was I supposed to react? I didn't go ballistic, but I was upset that he felt he couldn't tell me he had a change of plans.

So on the very next day, my boyfriend—whom I cherished for four and a half years—broke up with me in the most callous, cold-hearted manner, placing the blame solely on me and citing my inability to trust him as my offense. For the record, I never accused him of cheating on me. After all our time together, I never thought he would stray. I only wanted him to be truthful to me about whether he had feelings for the woman. When I asked him two weeks prior to the breakup if I should be worried about his friendship with the woman, he said, "No" and that was that. End of story. Well, believe me I tried to let it go. But his actions told me otherwise. After the dinner, something, call it female intuition, was telling me that even though he maintained they weren't having an affair, they shared a mutual attraction for each other and knowing that hurt like hell.

I couldn't believe that, after four and a half years of being together, he was going to break up with me over that. Other people in relationships have committed far worse crimes. My now ex said there were "other reasons" why he wanted to end our relationship but couldn't tell me because he didn't want me to get hurt. As if he hadn't hurt me enough already!

Bottom line was that, as I painfully look back, my ex—HE WHO SHALL NOT BE NAMED—kept finding fault in me. While he cared for and supported me in other ways, he fostered an abrasive brand of encouragement, a kind of "tough love." Instead of being happy that I got accepted into grad school and two years later graduated, all the while writing two novels and maintaining a full time job at the newspaper, he wasn't proud of me and didn't think much of my accomplishments. In other words, the things I cherished most about myself were the things he didn't deem worthwhile. He didn't seem to value or appreciate me even after I overlooked his flaws, focused on his good qualities, took care of his cats and his house while he was on vacation out of town or out of the country, cooked delicious, healthy vegetarian meals and loved him unconditionally from sunrise to sunset the whole time we were together.

The trouble is, I realize now, I didn't love myself enough. This was evident when I still continued to hang out with my ex post-breakup, at his urging. My friends made me see that he was only keeping me around as a "friend" solely for his benefit, not mine. He probably thought, by suddenly being nice to me, he was paying off his bad karmic debt. What was I getting out of it? I foolishly hoped for reconciliation, but as I knew that the woman was still very much in the picture, getting back together wasn't a possibility.

In fact, when I finally confronted him six weeks after the breakup whether he and the woman were together and he admitted it was headed in that direction, I felt my heart break yet again. Somehow, knowing this seemed much worse than when he broke up with me. This time around, I knew it was really over. Reality hit me, shattering my heart into a thousand splintered pieces.

What hurts isn't only that he rejected me, but that he quickly replaced me with someone else. I thought, like many of us who believe in everlasting love, that we were destined to be in this relationship for the long haul.

It also hurt even more to know that even though my ex knows how much I've been suffering, he has shown neither remorse nor compassion. He's disregarded my love for him and the years we spent together.

So my journey toward healing began. I had been in shock and denial for so long, even after I found out that the man I loved was with another woman. I wasn't just angry and depressed. In a way, I think I'm still in this phase and don't know how long I'll be here.

Nevertheless, I've learned it's where I need to be to get over this heartbreak eventually. After the breakup, I immediately sought comfort and advice from family and friends. Then I thought about the other people out there suffering from heartbreak. How could I reach out to them? I nixed the idea of organizing a heartbreak support group through Craigslist and thought about writing a Chick Lit novel about my experience.

But through my heartache, I rediscovered yoga and meditation and embraced spirituality again through my classes at a spiritually oriented yoga studio in Albany, California, located in an eclectic, diverse strip of businesses and homes east of San Francisco.

The result of finally embracing yoga as a spiritual practice has led me to the writing of this book and the mission to heal myself as I help others heal themselves.

You know the saying: "It gets worse before it gets better." Well, the aftermath of a breakup is the absolute worst time. The way to get through these first few days is to acknowledge your pain. You have a legitimate reason for grieving. You have suffered a real loss—the loss of your love and, in a sense, the loss of a bit of yourself. Don't let anyone tell you otherwise.

I spent the first few days crying, calling my friends and crying some more. In essence, I felt I endured two breakups—the first when my ex said we were over but we still hung out and I was still in denial. The second time was when I found out about him and his intention to pursue a relationship with the woman he initially insisted he didn't have romantic feelings for. The very thought of them being together, ironically, helped me realize my relationship was, in fact, over. Even though it hurt to know that he had replaced me so quickly with someone else, knowing he had someone new kept me from calling and seeing him. I was too hurt, too angry.

I typically respond to a breakup with a period of not eating and losing a lot of weight. Don't starve yourself. You need to eat. I had to force myself to eat. Ideally, you should be eating healthfully during this time but if that proves to be too much work for a heavy heart, at least eat something satisfying. Trust me, your stomach and your head will thank you.

You may feel like life isn't worth living and that the world is against you. During this initial shock and denial phase, let yourself feel what you want to feel—anger, sadness, despair. Incorporate the yogic principle of Truthfulness, or *Satya* in Sanskrit, as you open yourself to the grieving process. Stay true to yourself and your feelings. Now isn't the time to beat yourself up, give yourself a hard time or blame yourself.

You may not feel like getting up in the morning. You may prefer to stay in bed all day. You may not even feel like taking a shower. Tune into your body and its needs. Allow yourself to mourn, but listen to pangs of hunger and heed the scent of your malodor—your body's way of letting you know it needs an invigorating shower.

During this difficult stage, I'd already been taking yoga and made sure I attended regularly. If you haven't begun your yoga practice, now is a good time to. Even though it may feel like a yoga session or two may not be working at first, go to class anyway or practice on your own with a DVD. Chances are, whether you're a seasoned yogi or not, during the first stage of heartbreak, nothing will seem to be effective and you may not feel enthusiastic about anything. But hang in there. Tell yourself you have much to gain by continuing yoga, so keep at it.

Now would also be a good time to start meditating, although be forewarned—you will be distracted by thoughts about your ex and the pain that person inflicted on you. It's natural. Still, try to find some quiet time for deep breathing and reflection. If you only have five minutes, use it. Don't worry about whether you're meditating "improperly." There is no right or wrong way to meditate. All that is needed of you is your time, quiet space and ability to listen to yourself breathe.

Deep breathing can be your saving grace during moments of anxiety when you feel you've lost control or if a good or bad memory pops up. Instead of banishing that thought, memory or feeling, acknowledge it, without giving power to it. Continue to breathe. That feeling, thought or memory won't last forever.

Chapter 2:
Cry to Purify

Whenever my life is in turmoil, I usually turn to my spiritual literary guru, Iyanla Vanzant. She is the author of three books I own: *Acts of Faith*, *Faith in the Valley*, and *Until Today*.

In Iyanla's remarkable book, *Faith in the Valley* (they're all quite phenomenal), she describes a valley as "a life situation designed to teach us the character traits and spiritual virtues that are undeveloped and underdeveloped during our life experiences. Valleys help us to stretch, reach, and grow into our greatest potential."

In her book she further states: "Crying is a good thing to do in the valley because it clears the channels of communication. Crying purifies and cleanses."

For you, a time of pain or what Iyanla refers to as a "valley experience" could be a time of immense suffering or a time of healing. To embrace this time more fully to your benefit, you must be willing to make pain your friend, not your enemy.

The first step toward recovery is letting it all hang out—cry. There's nothing quite like a good cry to purge yourself of all the toxins from your relationship.

So cry whenever a good or bad memory pops up. Crying is the body's way of cleaning out your soul's closet of unwanted items so you can start anew. When the time is right to enter a new relationship, you won't be burdened with baggage from your previous relationship because you have taken the time to unload the anger, frustration, and grief through your tears, or so say my many friends.

Don't hold back when you're grieving. I've been moved to tears a few times during yoga, but not in a hysterical, bawling sort of way. Tears will well up a few times if I allow my mind to wander to a fond memory of me and my ex or if I think about the times he said some hurtful things. I try not to make a habit of this. Instead, I banish the good and bad thoughts away and concentrate on the pose at hand.

Sometimes a beautiful affirmation recited by a yoga instructor may move me to tears. I fully surrender myself to that in-the-moment vulnerability. I realize crying is a part of my recovery.

My former boyfriend hated seeing me or anyone else cry not because it upset him to see my anguish over such events as missing some of the kittens we fostered, but because he thought it was a sign of weakness.

I see crying as a sign of strength and the courage to be open to expression and intimacy. Tears shed in anguish liberate you from the hurt of the past. Tears are a sort of baptismal ritual, if you will, that allows you to be renewed in spirit and able to face challenges.

I know I feel a lot better after a good cry because I trust that it paves the way to enjoying an equally good laugh and tears of joy.

Chapter 3:
Put Your Heart on Paper

As hard as it may be, writing can be a powerful way to express your feelings and a safe way to put your thoughts on paper. Your journal can be your best friend during this difficult time. It won't judge you and is available 24/7. Journaling is a great way of tracking your progress toward recovery.

A bolder move would be to write a letter to your ex. This is a great way of purging all those feelings, laying it all out there, telling that person everything you didn't have the chance to tell him or her. An even braver move would be to send the letter to your ex—if you dare. But don't expect a response. When you write your letter, make it clear to yourself what your intentions are. It's perfectly fine to write an unedited version of your letter for yourself, one that you won't send.

If you do decide to write a letter to send, keep the tone respectful while still staying true to your feelings. As difficult as it may be to respect the person who broke your heart, you need to maintain your sense of dignity. Do not stoop down to your ex's level of nonchalance by thinking "Well, my ex didn't respect me, so why should I respect him or her?" You may not have yet mastered the art of loving yourself, but at least, respect yourself. If you don't think you can write a letter without lambasting your ex (even though he/she may deserve it) then maybe you shouldn't send it. Ask yourself, just how badly do I want him/her to know how I feel? The point of writing the letter is to serve your needs first and foremost, and to release all the negative toxins from your body, mind and spirit.

The point of sending the letter is to give you the closure you need. As you send the letter, bear in mind that whether your ex keeps the letter or not, those words are forever seared in your memory and that of your ex. Plus, if you were being a bitch on paper, there's always proof. You don't want your words to come back and haunt you.

I did say earlier to not expect a response if you send your letter. But admit it. We all want to know what our ex thinks on the other end. All I'm saying is to approach this letter writing activity, in fact, to approach this whole recovery process with no expectations. If you get a response, fine. If you don't, fine. You shouldn't send a letter to your ex to provoke a response anyway; the purpose is to let him or her know where you're coming from.

As of this writing, I have yet to receive acknowledgement from my ex regarding my own letter that I sent. But I'm not getting bent out of shape because I haven't received a response. He knows the kind of person he is and what he's capable of. If he genuinely had a compassionate heart, he'd know what to do.

Perhaps if the person who broke your heart feels the need to apologize or make peace at some point in the distant future, then give that person the opportunity to do so in his or her own time. Not yours.

In the meantime, you've done your part. Writing—and sending—your letter is an important first step toward recovery. Give yourself a hug. Then meditate on the detoxifying, good deed you just did.

Chapter 4:
Gratitude

Meditate on this: How many times have we heard the advice "Cultivate an attitude of gratitude?"

All too often. But how often do we actually do it? How often should we feel grateful?

Every second.

The aftermath of a breakup really quickly puts things in perspective. If we're lucky, we find that we are surrounded by a support network of loving family and friends. Let each of them know how thankful you are for their love and support. Now would also be a good time to befriend yourself. Tell yourself "Thank you for getting me this far, for taking each day as it comes."

If you believe in a higher power—God, the Divine, Spirit, whomever—thank that source as well for getting you through another day. It doesn't matter who or what you believe in. What's important is showing gratitude.

One way to do that is through yoga. As you practice yoga, you're cultivating an attitude of gratitude that you will hopefully take with you in and out of yoga class.

First, be grateful for taking yourself or a friend or family member with you to yoga. Be thankful for the means of getting you there. Show appreciation to your body for doing the poses. Even though you may not do the challenging poses or asanas, still thank yourself for having the courage to prevent yourself from getting injured and for being honest with yourself for knowing your limits. You can't force yourself to stop loving your ex in the same way you can't force yourself to do the headstand when you're not physically ready.

Even though you may not do so out loud, at least silently thank the others in yoga class for sharing this experience with you. Everyone has their own reasons for practicing yoga just as everyone has their own hang-ups and challenges in life. Take a moment to honor those who are going through difficulties as you are and know you're not alone.

Thank your yoga instructor. If you have an instructor who emphasizes yoga as a spiritual practice— thus honoring its ancient origins—as well as a physical practice, then consider yourself lucky. I've had the honor of practicing with a wonderful yoga teacher in Albany who includes positive affirmations and also points out the benefits of poses in her classes.

Your yoga instructor can be your spiritual mentor and guide, if you wish. Yoga instructors, no matter how poetically smooth they may move on the mat, no matter how graceful they may look while in those challenging poses, are still human beings who stress and hurt like the rest of us. Having a yoga teacher certification status may not grant one an enlightened state of mind 24/7, but generally, yoga instructors have studied the spiritual history, tradition and philosophy of yoga and armed with that knowledge, they can best guide you on the path toward healing yourself. So thank them for their teachings.

If you haven't started doing so already, take the time to savor your surroundings on your way to yoga class by thanking each bird, each driver, each pedestrian, each tree, and each cat or dog or squirrel you pass by. Be grateful for everything you see. Yes, even the not-so-good stuff.

You need to realize that it is in pain and suffering that we'll eventually grow, heal and love ourselves.

After coming back from a yoga retreat she attended, a yoga instructor said something that struck me: "Be thankful for even the bad things." In pain, we find truth. In suffering, we discover we have a lot to be grateful for. Take time to start and end each day sending a message of gratitude.

Remind yourself in times of grief and despair that you have something to live for—all you have to do is look around you, look at your blessings and savor all you are thankful for.

ॐ

Chapter 5:
Tender Loving Care

By incorporating yogic habits off the mat as well as on, you're well on the path toward healing. Yes, it's a tedious journey, but it's worth the effort in the long run.

Start by adopting the yogic concept of Purity, or *Saucha* in Sanskrit. Simply put, this purity habit means treating yourself with a lot of TLC. This means making sure that whatever you put on and into your body is healthy for you as can be.

Even though we may feel like crap inside after a breakup, we know we are working on resolving the issues our inner selves are facing on the road to healing.

But we don't have to look like crap on the outside. While it may be easy to let ourselves go during this time of heartbreak and misery, we must take pride in our appearance. We want to send a message out to the world, to our ex (whether he/she is watching) and most of all, to ourselves, that we are doing and looking our best despite the circumstances.

Now isn't the time to play a martyr by showing up for work unshowered and unshaven. Taking time to pamper yourself is therapeutic. So, go ahead, get that haircut, scalp treatment, foot and/or body massage, manicure, pedicure and savor the experience guilt-free.

You deserve it! It's about time someone took care of you. That someone is you.

While massage therapy has obvious healing benefits, one way to look at yoga and meditation is giving your body and your mind a massage.

When your heart's been broken and you're hunched over from despair or fear of getting hurt again, know that there are heart-opening yoga poses that physically enable you to breathe your way toward emotional freedom thus carving the path to healing and opening your heart again. Ask for your yoga instructor's help on attempting these poses and don't expect a quick cure. Healing yourself through yoga, just like the mending of a broken heart, takes time.

Some poses that may help include spinal twists, Camel pose and yoga mudra—hands in prayer position behind your back and folding forward while sitting with legs crossed. These poses encourage you to open up your chest to invite the healing essence in. To ensure proper form and to prevent injury, seek the assistance of a yoga instructor as you attempt these heart-opening poses.

The Yoga of Food

This is a good time to take care of your insides as well as your outsides. This means nourishing yourself with healthy food. When you've been rejected and replaced, it's easy to think that the person who dumped you deserved better. You must know—this isn't true. When we allow negative thoughts to consume us, we accept this as the truth when the real truth is, we're no longer with that person because WE deserve better. We just haven't realized it yet because the pain is still so raw.

Don't give into this thought. A self-defeatist, self-pitying attitude won't help you. While it may be tempting to dive into junk food and eat your way through sorrow, you can't afford to perpetuate the absurd notion that you were dumped because you weren't good enough. Typically, people who get rejected either overeat or don't eat at all. I tend to do the latter.

Choose whole grain food options—wheat or multigrain bread, pasta and brown rice. Dive into the salad bar. Whip up creative smoothies using fruits that are in season. I've found solace in my neighborhood Farmers Market where I know that through the vegetables and fruit I purchase, I'm supporting the local farmers, the environment and myself. Also remember to hydrate yourself. Give coconut water a try. It's a natural beverage filled with potassium and electrolytes, but be forewarned—it's an acquired taste.

Nourishing yourself with healthy, preferably organic food, is one of the most loving acts you can bestow on yourself. Someone has hurt you—why would you want to hurt yourself even further? Focus the aftermath of a breakup on damage control. Damage has been done to your heart, mind and spirit. You need to repair the damage by giving your body, mind and spirit—the whole package—some TLC. Think of yourself as a car that needs major repairs, and then continue on with regular maintenance because caring for yourself shouldn't be a one-time experience.

Move to Move On

Another path toward recovery is through exercise. I prefer to run and walk outdoors so I can be in touch with nature. It's the most organic way to stay in shape.

Not only do I get a huge dose of fresh air (believe me, your lungs will thank you, so get your butt out there!) I find much enjoyment from greeting the birds, ducks, people and their dogs and the feral cats at a creek trail near my home. There's nothing quite like communing with the natural world. As the sun and wind caress your face, you'll never feel more alive.

You are What You Wear

Once you've impressed upon yourself the importance of feeling good on the inside as well as the outside, consider dressing the part. While it may be tempting to take on the self-defeatist "I (crappily) dress the way I (crappily) feel," you won't be doing yourself any good. After an invigorating shower, cast your closet door or drawers wide open and give your clothes a much-needed scrutiny. Ask yourself, "Which clothes look the most flattering on me and which ones don't?" Give away clothes that don't flatter your body. Don't get attached to any one clothing item. If it doesn't work, toss it out!

I have actually begun to take pride in my appearance everywhere I go. This has little to do with attracting the opposite sex and more to do with feeling good about yourself. Whether you're going out with friends, going to a party, or going grocery shopping, it's a confidence booster knowing you're looking your best.

When attending yoga class, it's important to wear comfortable clothes. But stretch your yogic self (no pun intended) further by choosing flattering, perhaps even trendy yoga tank tops and pants. Experiment with different colors and designs. Don't shy away from a hint of spandex as it accentuates the curves of your body and moves along with you as your body flows from pose to pose. Looking great on the outside helps you feel awesome on the inside.

Your body and your mind are works of art and deserve a lot of TLC.

Chapter 6:
Practice Makes (Im)Perfect

Even though we often hear the saying "Practice makes perfect," and long to heed this advice when mastering a yoga pose, the premise of yoga, much like the premise of living, is that nobody's perfect.

Instead, it's better to approach life with the attitude of "I did or I am doing the best that I can." I like to view this whole concept as "striving for imperfection." There's no pressure to be perfect to satisfy anyone's or society's standards. As long as you're happy with yourself and what you did, that's all that matters.

Taking on the pressure to be perfect on the yoga mat as well as beyond the mat will no doubt invite disaster into your life. "Perfecting" or "mastering" a yoga pose doesn't mean stretching your limbs out as far and as wide as your yoga instructor. What yoga is encouraging you to do is to approach your practice with self compassion and contentment, or *Samtosha*, in Sanskrit. This means striving to go into a pose in the best possible way you can manage without physical or emotional strain. Go as far as you can go without subjecting yourself to injury. Do not, I repeat, do not chastise yourself for not assuming a pose as well as the yogi next to you. Yoga practice, in class and in life, isn't about comparing yourself to others. It's not about putting yourself down. Most likely, in our past relationships, we may have experienced our share of being put down by our former partners. The last thing we need is to be condescending to ourselves. Thou shall not covet thy neighbor's "perfect" yoga form. This is going against the yogic precept of nonstealing, *Asteya* in Sanskrit. You can't go through life coveting another person's career, boyfriend or yoga pose.

We must be proud of our own bodies, as imperfect as they are, and of the accomplishments of our imperfect selves. We must learn to embrace our flaws as well as those of our loved ones. By flaws I mean those endearing qualities—beauty marks, shortness, tallness, inquisitiveness, tendency to ramble, etc., that make us who we are.

My ex criticized me constantly about my figure and size. Apparently, a size six was "too big" for him and even when I dropped back to my "normal" size four, it didn't seem to make any difference.

He thought my attending grad school was a waste of time and he said he didn't think I worked hard enough even though I'd not only attended grad school full time, I also maintained my full-time career as a journalist and wrote two novels in a two to three-year period. He criticized me for going on an hour-long morning jog, claiming it wasn't rigorous enough of a workout. He criticized me for not being an "outdoor girl," even though I preferred working out on the trail instead of inside a gym.

Was he perfect? Absolutely not! He had his share of flaws and that's putting it mildly. But I saw past those flaws and preferred to focus on his qualities and appreciated his good-natured side. He instead preferred to magnify my flaws. In fact, the very things he criticized me about were the very things I cherished—my writing, my body, my whole self. But I obviously wasn't doing a good job of honoring and respecting myself as I put up with his criticisms. Now, I don't have to anymore because the only opinion that matters is my own.

And I realized that my ex-boyfriend's criticisms were untrue and that I should not allow other people to make me feel bad about myself.

Through constant practice of yoga and meditation, I've learned to love and accept myself, flaws and all. The saying "You are perfect as you are," began to make sense to me.

Chapter 7:
Love Yourself
to Heal Yourself

Self love and not being afraid to face your fears and your flaws is the path toward healing. Learn to cultivate a genuine belief that you deserve to be happy by not counting on outside sources—namely another person—to make you happy. Rely on no one but yourself.

Yoga and meditation encourage you to not only look within but to be gentle, patient and loving with yourself. Aside from practicing the yogic precept of contentment and appreciating who you really are, infuse your life with another important yogic principle—*Tapas*, or self discipline. This means honoring yourself by practicing yoga and meditation frequently. I admit there are days when I feel a bit lazy going to yoga class. Then I remind myself, would I go through a whole day without eating or sleeping? I may not attend yoga class every day but I make a point to do some basic poses at home like standing or seated forward bends, stretching, Butterfly pose, Cat/Cow pose and Downward Dog.

Yoga encourages us to explore our bodies and minds, engaging us in *Svadhyaya* or self study. You should always strive to discover who you really are, not just through hobbies and your career.

As you move through each posture, you will gain an appreciation of your strength and the flexibility and power of your body. With constant practice, you will marvel at what your body is capable of doing and applaud yourself for accomplishing the pose to the best of your efforts.

Concentrating on the pose and your movements in class trains you to focus on the present, an important aspect to a successful yoga and meditation practice.

As yoga inspires you to rediscover your body, meditation will encourage you to explore your mind. Strive to start each day with a positive affirmation. Some examples from my deck of Power Thought cards by Louise L. Hay would be: "All is well in my world," and "Life mirrors my every thought. As I keep my thoughts positive, life brings to me only good experiences."

Feel free to make your own affirmations. I normally affirm: "Peace, joy and love dwell within me— I am healing," an affirmation I've latched onto post-breakup. "I am a beautiful, intelligent, confident, and strong woman," has always been a favorite pick-me-up on days when I'm not feeling my best.

If you're anything like I used to be—relying on the words and actions of your partner (the one who ultimately rejected you) to make you happy, you're in need of some serious and quick reprogramming.

Self study includes treating yourself to a plethora of personal growth literature such as reading the Yoga Sutras. So get thee to the nearest self-empowerment books section. There are several helpful books out there that are inspiring as well as life transforming, assuming you actually put theory into practice. *Living Yoga*, written by Christy Turlington-Burns, gave me my very first introduction to yoga as a spiritual practice and even with my ever-expanding yoga library, Christy's book continues to inspire me. Along with her book, I have included a list of recommended books at the end of this guide.

In addition to books, attending workshops and retreats can be helpful. Although I try to meditate a few minutes daily, attending meditation workshops and classes keeps me attuned to my practice and receptive to new ways of thinking positively and being still in the present. I also receive the additional support of like-minded, spiritually seeking individuals at the Mindfulness Meditation group, led by meditation teacher Wendy Beckerman, which meets at the Pinole Library near my home. One of the best things about these sessions is that they're free.

Loving yourself is the best antidote to heartbreak. The thing to remember is: You can't just love yourself when things are going great. It's important to love yourself even more when things fall apart. And when they do, trust yourself to get through this and trust that life will bring you the just reward for all the lessons you've learned through this difficult experience.

Part Two

The Real World:
Anchoring Yourself
in the Present

*Rejecting another human being simply because
they are human, has become a collective
neurosis. People ask, 'When will my soul mate
get here?' But praying for the right person is
useless if we're not ready to receive him. Our
soul mates are human beings, just like we are,
going through the normal processes of growth.
No one is ever 'finished.'*

—Marianne Williamson
<u>A Return to Love</u>

Chapter 8:
You are Going Now-Here

The pain of a broken heart may often leave a person feeling disoriented, wandering aimlessly with a feeling she or he is going nowhere.

The truth is, if you remain still for a few moments, you are actually headed somewhere. You are NOW HERE. Here and now, this very second, is where you should be. So, if you are experiencing emotional pain this moment, be here right now with your pain. Yes, the point of yoga, meditation and living is to be free from pain and suffering, yet to reach that destination of total bliss, you've first got to ride the wave. Make pain your friend, instead of your enemy. Do it right now. Then, you'll soon be going places.

At the onset of heartbreak it is natural to review your past actions, go through them with a fine tooth comb, analyze situations and burden yourself with things you thought you could have done, words you should have or shouldn't have said. The truth is, everything that happened in the past is what it is—in the past. It should stay there.

Everything that happened then was meant to happen. What's happening now is meant to be. Hard as it is to believe, where you are right now is where you should be. Instead of thinking that you're being punished or being forced to pay a bad karmic debt, try to embrace this pain as an opportunity to change and grow.

A friend of mine told me two days after my breakup that I should consider myself lucky. Of course, at the time as I was tearfully lamenting over what I thought I did to piss off my ex, I couldn't fathom feeling I was the luckiest person alive. I felt anything but that. All I could think of was, how dare he break up with me, after I had been so good to him? If anything, I could've left him a long time ago when he began to show his less than desirable side, to put it mildly. Amid my anguish, however, my friend's words rang out loud and clear even though I didn't quite understand what she meant at the time: "He is setting you free. He has carried issues his whole life that he's dumped on you. It's not you, it's him."

I thought she was just saying that, especially that last part, to make me feel better. But another friend pointed out very succinctly six agonizing weeks later when I found out I'd been hastily replaced: "He is her problem now."

Even though my friends meant what they said and weren't only saying those words to make me feel better, these truths were hard to digest. I kept pouring over how unhappy he said he was and somehow repeatedly pointed my fingers at myself as the root of his unhappiness.

It took several empowering yoga and meditation sessions for me to realize that the fault didn't lie solely with me. He failed to hold himself accountable for his own unhappiness. I learned a long time ago that couples should complement not complete each other and that it was better if love flowed unconditionally. Therefore, it wasn't my fault he wasn't happy.

We all have the capacity to ignite happiness in ourselves by tapping that divine source of joy within us. One huge way to achieve this is through meditation.

When we meditate, we are calling forth our innate sense of wisdom that dwells within that has lain dormant because we've chosen to rely on outside sources to fuel our souls. I'm not suggesting that you cease asking advice from family or friends. In fact, by all means, do reach out to them during this time of crisis. However, bear in mind that the ultimate answers lie within, waiting to be drawn out through the power of connecting with yourself.

Try sitting still in a comfortable position quietly for as long as you can. As you settle into your seat, listen only to yourself inhaling and exhaling. Then silently ask the burning question you urgently want answered. An example could be, "What am I learning from this experience?" Assert to yourself that the universe has especially chosen you to go through this experience so that you may emerge recharged and recalibrated and ready to take on whatever life throws your way.

But as long as you allow yourself to be enslaved by bad memories you will remain chained to your past, thereby preventing yourself from moving beyond what has already happened, which you don't have the power to change anyway. You must accept this and the sooner you do, the better off you'll be.

Some meditation techniques I've found to be helpful in anchoring myself in the present include concentrating on my breathing and listening to sounds near or far. Whether calming or jarring, they're the sounds happening now—a car honking, a siren of a police car, a dog barking, children outside playing. While ordinarily when you meditate you should tune out these sounds, for the sole purpose of anchoring yourself in present time, it may benefit you to tune into the beauty of your present acoustic environment. This way, you know for sure these sounds are, in fact, occurring this very second—there's no doubt about it.

If you're meditating outside, at a park for instance, feel free to open your eyes and enjoy the scenery around you and appreciate everything you see. Just like observing the sounds, try to take in every color, shape and form of things around you, even people. Tell yourself, "There's nothing quite like this second, this moment."

A favorite in-the-moment mantra I love to use often is "Be here now." I especially like to use this whenever I'm experiencing something positive like cuddling a kitten, feeling empowered by Warrior pose, enjoying gelato at a piazza in front of the Pantheon on a recent trip to Rome, teaching a creative writing class, or being engrossed in a favorite book.

One thing that may be preventing you from being in the moment might be thinking about the good times when your ex still loved and cherished you. Again, it's time to face the facts. Where is your lover now? Not with you. You may be alone but being alone and single doesn't translate to being undesirable or miserable. Gone are the days when your lover said or did things to make your heart sing. You know what? You're still around. You've survived the initial trauma of the breakup. Now, it's entirely up to you.

You have the power to create new and lasting memories starting now and you don't need another mate to do that. Begin by seeking out meditation workshops that offer various ways of connecting with yourself. Experiment with different yoga styles and teachers. Make new friends. Take up new hobbies. Join a common interest group—knitting and crocheting, rock climbing, cooking class, or creative writing class, a movie club or book club—or better yet, start your own—the more unique the concept, the better for your confidence. Observe your pulse quicken in anticipation of all the new people you'll meet and the new skills you'll learn. You are living your life, even as you're still recovering from heartbreak, because life pauses for no one.

Chapter 9:
Minding Your Manners

What do you do once you're finally in the present? Stay here!

One of the most powerful ways of appreciating today is through minding your manners. This means observing, paying attention to and being mindful of the manner in which you think, speak, eat and walk—all your actions. By gently, not critically, scrutinizing your every move, you're keeping yourself in the here and now.

Practicing mindfulness is a tender way of appreciating life's simplest pleasures. So don't just savor the rare, extraordinary moments like viewing an Alaskan glacier or scaling Mt. Kilimanjaro (if you're ever so lucky to experience these occasions). Learn to find beauty in the ordinary—the softness of a rose petal, the warmth of the sun on your face, the sound of a cat purring. The ordinary can be extraordinary if you make it so.

Let every detail come alive in the moment—the sound of "Moonlight Sonata" on a piano, the way your flannel pajamas caress your body. Make every facet of every moment or sensory experience count.

Being human, you'll find yourself straying from the present from time to time. Sometimes when I am in the present, I often find myself stuck in the wrong present moment—my ex's. Wondering how and what he's doing and who he's with only brings me more pain and I can't do that to myself. The only present moment I should be concerned with is my own.

Don't worry about his or her present moment or what she or he will do in the future. Your only concern should be yourself. I can't emphasize this enough.

Recognize that, although this person has hurt you, if you're still hurting now long after the breakup, you're only hurting yourself. I know you can't rush getting over someone you've loved—it can't be forced. All I'm suggesting is you have the power to focus on what you can do now to make yourself feel better. The longer you keep yourself entrenched in the past, the harder it is to move on. Even if you still communicate with your former partner (because you still work with, still need to divide property with or share custody with that person) and what she or he says or does still affects you; remember, it's because you're letting it affect you. You're giving your ex power over you. Don't do that to yourself.

You can choose to let that comment or action go—or, better yet, let that person go. Let go. Do it for yourself, not just for the meantime, but forever. You have nothing to lose and only yourself to gain.

Being mindful also means resisting the temptation to call your ex and give that person a piece of your mind when you know better than to do that. There are healthier ways to vent your anger and disappointment.

Don't worry about whether this person will resurface in your life in the future. Don't worry or think about things that haven't happened yet or may never happen. Stay in the now.

Chapter 10:
Journaling

One effective way of staying in the present is through recording your thoughts, feelings and accomplishments on paper. By keeping a journal, you're also tracking your emotional as well as physical progress.

Writing about your experiences in yoga class provides you with an in-depth introspection of precisely what you were thinking and feeling while assuming a pose. Journaling gently reminds you of the impermanence in life. While every day is different, you are to cherish each day whether or not you accomplish something. The attempt of a challenging yoga pose is a blessing in and of itself. The fact that you made the effort is sufficient in itself. Applaud your effort to even show up to class on a day you were tempted to go shopping or stay at home and surf the Internet.

Journaling isn't just for recording the good things. By only acknowledging the positive, you're not making an accurate account of your life. You'd be cheating yourself of the purpose of journaling—keeping a written testament of how you made it through from heartbreak to happiness.

A journal entry should include both good days and off days when you're distracted during yoga class, the times you lost your balance doing tree pose, the moment you caught yourself envying another yogi's flawless and seemingly effortless crane pose. Remind yourself constantly that it's not easy to hold your entire body off the floor with your two hands.

Just like life, there are good and bad days. Journaling is proof that you'll survive the choppy waters of life and the turbulence of negative emotions.

Keeping a journal is a means of regularly communicating and sharing in a nonjudgmental way with your most intimate, most precious friend—yourself. So the words you write must benefit, not hurt, you.

Your journal will help you determine when it's time to give up forcing yourself to do a difficult pose and whether you should try a different yoga style or instructor. While it's perfectly fine to keep a file of your journal on your computer, I believe there's something empowering and personal about the communion of pen to paper. Journaling keeps you attuned to your body, mind and spirit, connecting all three essences of you through the power of the pen. If you're able to acquire guided yoga journals, even better. Otherwise, blank journals work just fine.

I don't usually write in my yoga journal every day but I try to at least write an entry after every class. You should consider keeping a meditation journal as well. This way you remain aware of how your mind, body and spirit benefit from your practice.

Attempt to write using a stream-of-consciousness technique, a flow of writing that's raw, in the moment, uninhibited. This means pay no attention to grammar, punctuation or your analytical mind and try not to succumb to the temptation to edit your thoughts. Remember, this writing is for your eyes only, and its intent is to heal yourself.

Here's an example of a journal entry, unedited and unabashed, which is of course the preferred and nonjudgmental way of communicating with yourself. This was written during the very early stages of my heartbreak. I tried to be more aware of my poses and emotions, noticing their existence with the intention toward self-acceptance without being critical.

April 22, 2009

Since I hadn't been eating, I was worried about my energy level as well as my state of mind. Would I do the poses okay? Would I be too distracted? How was I going to focus? After all, this was the first session since the truth (about my ex and the woman) came out.

My forward bends started out stiff and I kept vowing to practice this at home everyday. Getting better doing sitting bends, focusing on a leg at a time. Each time I succeed, I congratulate myself. Just like life's challenges, progress takes time.

The Butterfly pose is always a relaxing pose in which I feel most womanly. My Sun Salutations weren't seamless, but the point was, I did them. There's something to be said about bringing palms down to the heart center. The very act brings about power and peace. Tree poses could be better, but I keep remembering what a former yoga instructor of mine once said: 'Inability or ability to do balance postures reflect how you balance your life.' So, I intend to practice balance to invite more balance in my life.

Chair pose variations were not at all challenging and I was told these poses were great for the knees. As I attempted to balance on each foot, distractive thoughts took precedence over concentrating in the moment.

Warrior variation pose with hands flexed and leaning from side to side, any Warrior pose, to me, signifies power and strength. I feel I can conquer my challenges in life when I assume Warrior poses.

Triangle variations always make me feel like I'm going to tip over, but I have to focus and learn to steady my body and my thoughts and eliminate distractions.

Understandably, I'd been distracted—thoughts about the past as well as the future kept creeping up. Thoughts about my ex's not loving me anymore made me momentarily sad, but I snapped out of it as I didn't want to miss the teacher's instructions. She and I talked a bit about my heartbreak and how yoga's been my lifeline—my key to surviving and coping. I heard about statistics that showed that friendships and interaction with an ex so soon after a breakup only perpetuates pain. Boy, were those stats right!

The Albany yoga teacher kept affirmations on long white strips of paper in a bowl, which I picked through some days after yoga class. The affirmation I randomly chose for that day which I glued to the page of my journal dated April 22, 2009 appropriately read: "I am never narrowed or embittered by difficulties, but rather lifted to a new level of understanding and inner freedom."

In the previous entry, each journal page encouraged me to break down my observations pose-by-pose and how I felt when I did them; however you don't have to do it this way. What's important is that you jot down your emotions and thoughts, good or bad. Notice the difference between the previous journal entry and the next two:

May 11, 2010

*I'd wanted to attend Angie's class for a while now. Aside
from Sarah's class, Angie's was the only other class where I got a
dose of spirituality.*

*So, true to my yogic spirit—I'm trying not to lay a guilt
trip on myself for not visiting the yoga journal pages for so long.
Instead, I plan to slowly go back and read over exercises and try to
get the full benefit of this endeavor. After all, I preach the holy
goodness of journaling to my students every chance I get.*

*Some of what Angie said at the conclusion of class: You
never know until you try what you can achieve. See what you can
do—even if it isn't perfect. When practicing yoga, you needn't be
calm always. Be true to who/what you are (depressed/frustrated).
Trying to achieve perfect calm is not honest. Consider this: Maybe
this is all there is (in life). And this is enough.*

Time heals wounds, as they say, and while I
wasn't completely over my ex, this next journal entry is
proof of how far my emotional state has progressed:

May 23, 2010

*I have to be honest. I was so afraid at first to attend Yoga
in the Park at Civic Park. Not that I hadn't ever practiced
outdoors, but I was more apprehensive about the possibility that
my ex may be there. After all, this type of outdoor activity was
something he would attend. What would I do? What would I say
if I encountered him? Yet, I had to be there to observe the class
and interview people for my newspaper story. Plus, I was eager to
practice yoga outdoors on such a beautiful, warm spring day.*

And I'm glad I did. After it was apparent my ex wasn't going to be there, I started to relax. People placed their mats in a circle, Mandala-style, just as Sarah had us do once in class.

Though Sarah didn't wear a microphone, her voice lifted with the wind and soared, soothed and caressed like the gentle breeze that day.

Despite the blazing sun, we flowed to the beat of world drum music. How liberating it was to be outside!

Sarah asked us to set an intention and mine was my usual one: May peace, joy love and happiness dwell within me—I am safe. I am healing.

I felt my spirits rise as I lifted my face to the heavens. How blue and beautiful the sky was! How grounding it was to do Downward Dog on the grass—to firmly root hands and bare feet to the ground—to connect with Mother Earth! While the sun was at my back, I could feel its energy. We kept flowing from one pose to the next as we generated heat from our bodies, from the sun.

Sarah had us squat and do Chair poses in true Sarah fashion as she asked that our movements be watery, our squats should pulse, pulse, pulse!

The sun seared right through me during Savasana. But what an achievement—yoga outdoors! I've done standing poses before at Hidden Lakes Park in Martinez, known to me fondly as Yoga Lake, with my tennis shoes, but this was my first actual yoga class on the grass with my mat. I did interviews for the story afterward—even work didn't affect my mood. No ex at this event! I felt relieved and free!

Chapter 11:
Walking (or Running)
in Spirit

As I mentioned earlier, walking or running outdoors to relieve stress has been, for me, the best possible way to connect with nature and my divine self.

Before my breakup, I had been walking and jogging nearly every day for about a year so my post-breakup, stress-relieving walks came naturally. For me, the best time to walk is early morning—I can start the day off right, get some exercise and fresh air and clear my mind to get myself prepared for the day ahead.

I've also been using this time for prayer and meditation. Prayer connects me to the Spirit as I express gratitude for the gift of the day, my life, my family, and my friends. It goes something like this: "Thank you for this day and all its possibilities. Please help me to show my love in any way that I can and please help me to use the special talents that I've been given."

Included in my special intentions are guidance for myself and my loved ones in times of joy and turmoil. I've also asked that all the homeless pets find loving, forever homes. Speaking of pets, I had the opportunity to practice Karma Yoga, the type of yoga practice that involves serving others, courtesy of my regular communion with nature. My sister and I rescued a stray kitten that lived in a drainpipe at the creek near our home. The kitten would approach us purring, cuddling us, and hoping to get some food, and we'd always provide for her needs. But as she was no longer feral and her chance of survival outdoors was slim, we decided she had to be rescued. She deserved a home where she would be loved and cared for. At the time of this writing, she's at the home of a friend who fosters kittens.

So you never know what kinds of fortunate circumstances, ideas, thoughts, and feelings will cross your external and internal path as you take your spiritual practice outdoors. Churches, temples or sanctuaries aren't the only sacred places. Plus, there's something to be said about spirituality in motion.

I first learned the practice of walking meditation during a retreat at Buddha Gate Monastery. While sitting meditation connects me intimately to myself through the breath, walking meditation gives me the option of feeling the earth beneath my feet as I mindfully take each step. As I breathe, cool air fills my lungs and energizes me.

You can devote your entire walk or run to meditation. I usually jog a few laps around the nearby creek or around the nearest park first, and then I devote the last two laps to meditation. As I walk in meditation, I concentrate only on the present and try to cast my thoughts aside. My mantra: "Think positive thoughts or no thoughts." It's one or the other. Your body may be moving, but your mind can't be racing. I say strive to think about nothing at all but if that's too difficult and if you're going to think about something, it might as well be about something positive.

If you're wondering how walking meditation can be beneficial, consider this—sitting for a long period of time in meditation, although great for your emotional health and peace of mind, can cause a strain on your legs. It's nice to have the option to meditate as you keep your blood circulating and your heart pumping. What better way to do that than going for a meditative walk?

While the pace of your walk may vary, the key thing is to still your mind as your body remains in motion. What a great feeling it is to be the master of your mind and body as you commune with Spirit.

ॐ

Chapter 12:
**The Five 'Ws'
of Yoga & Meditation**

Who:

The exciting thing about practicing yoga and meditation is that you can begin anew anytime, anywhere with anyone, whether you're a novice or a seasoned yogi. One way to approach your practice with a fresh perspective is by practicing with different yoga instructors or meditation teachers.

You can continue to practice yoga and meditation with the same person you've always been practicing with while trying out new styles. I've found that when I really like a teacher, I tend to become too attached. This attachment, I believe, has pros and cons. Practicing with the same instructor can encourage you to attend regularly as you may be comfortable with your instructor's teaching style. But being too comfortable might prevent you from growing. This is why I suggest experimenting with different classes while still staying loyal to your regular class.

On the other hand, the same instructor you've been attending classes with may have gotten to know you, your preferences and body's limitations. In this case, staying with the same instructor who's nurtured your physical as well as spiritual growth may be more to your benefit. Trust your instincts as to what's best for you.

A yoga teacher I know whose advice I treasure offers this:

> *Yoga is meant to be a lifetime path and commitment, a yogic lifestyle in combination with the practice of the poses and meditation techniques. You can usually sense this about an instructor or discover it by speaking to them or by listening to their comments in class. They may write about it in their brochure or Web site. You can see it in how they treat other students and in the vibration of the studio itself. There's a tangible healing energy in the room that you can feel when you're calm enough. That energy is generated not only by the teacher but it is also an alchemy of the ongoing practice of the group year after year. The study and practice of the philosophy of yoga may begin long before a Hatha Yoga teacher-training program and continue throughout life for those who embrace it on a deeper level.*

She goes on to say that choosing a teacher who can help you is very individual—there is a special chemistry that draws and uplifts you. It's an aspect of the class that is extremely important but often ignored. Each teacher is unique and has something special to contribute to others in this world.

What:

There are different styles of yoga just as there are different meditation techniques. Give yourself the chance to try a variety of yoga styles—examples include Vinyasa, a graceful and vigorous practice with flowing movements as well as Anusara and Iyengar yoga which both emphasize precise body alignment, although Anusara provides a dose of spirituality; and in addition, there is Ashtanga yoga which involves rigorous, athletic poses.

First, try to figure out what your purpose and intentions are for practicing yoga. Bear in mind that traditionally, yoga is a spiritual practice and not a religion, so don't worry about yoga conflicting with your beliefs, whatever they are. That said, you should expect to at least get a sprinkling of enlightenment during class, some words of wisdom, and comfort that can be applied universally.

Realize that while yoga can be physical exercise, it's more than that. Hopefully, as you're attempting challenging poses, you are learning and appreciating yourself in the process.

I appreciate the meditative aspect of yoga. For me, the perfect class is one that combines a healthy dose of yoga and meditation with an emphasis on connecting with the breath and mastering breathing techniques which can have physical as well as emotional benefits. I've heard that self-guided meditation using audio CDs may also be effective.

When:

How often to practice is a question yogis and meditation practitioners ask. The simple answer is—as often as your schedule allows. To achieve maximum benefits, whether you're recovering from heartbreak or not, practice should be a daily habit.

If you can't attend yoga class regularly, you can practice at home. I sometimes start and end my days with a few simple poses—forward bends, Half Moon pose, Warrior, Yoga Mudra, hip rotations, head and shoulder rolls. I usually do these standing yoga poses during a jogging break and after walking or jogging.

Poses that involve lying or sitting on a mat or on the carpet at home include supine twists, legs on the wall, Butterfly pose and Pigeon pose. Time devoted to meditation may vary depending on your schedule. I usually find time before going to bed. I try to devote at least 15 to 20 minutes of much deserved quiet time before surrendering to a peaceful slumber. Starting out your day with 5 to 10 minutes of meditation may be ideal for you, even if you are the get-up-and-go type. Clearing your mind and filling your lungs with oxygen first thing in the morning does wonders for the body and soul.

Where:

To practice yoga at the gym or at a yoga studio? That is the question each yogi faces. If you're already a member of the gym then it's worth your while to attend classes there and take full advantage of your gym membership. I first started taking yoga at a gym but was fortunate that it took place in a soundproof room. My other gym yoga experiences weren't so serene. One class was held out in the open alongside the various weight training machines as people were using them.

It wasn't until I attended yoga at a local community center that I felt I could focus more on my practice. Of course, taking a class at a gym, with all its distractions, could be a personal challenge to take on—an exercise on tuning out the outside world and turning inward.

Practicing at a yoga studio can boost your experience with the spiritual realm. Yoga studios are designed to enhance the complete practice of uniting mind, body and spirit. Studios are generally equipped with pillows, blankets, dim lighting, candles and meditative music. Some may even infuse a bit of incense. I like the scents emanating from incense and essential oils as they may enhance the sacred sensory experience but I don't favor perfume while attending yoga and meditation classes. It's not a good idea to wear perfume to yoga class. If scents bother you, take this into serious consideration as it can make or break your experience. Ditto for the gym. If you find the odor of sweat bothersome, then nix yoga at the gym.

Don't rule out the option of practicing outdoors. If you can lay out your mat on a deck overlooking the ocean, on the beach, on grass at a park, you may do standing yoga poses. I don't find this limiting to my experience at all. In fact, being outdoors enhances the experience. On the days I walk on trails near a lake, I make it a point to stop and do standing poses right near the water. As I move into forward bends, Warrior pose and balance poses like Tree or Dancer pose, I focus on the soft ripples of the lake a few feet before me. Practicing near any body of water provides an instant feeling of peace. Since I frequently practice at this lake, I have now fondly dubbed this place my "Yoga Lake." You, too, can find a sacred space to call your own.

The great thing about meditation is it's a portable stress reliever and soul enhancer—it can be practiced anywhere. From your bed to your car (parked, of course), to a park, or near the ocean, you can meditate anywhere. Once in a while, I like to go to Buddha Gate Monastery in Lafayette to meditate outdoors at their hilltop gazebo. A temple or sanctuary will also suffice. While I may not regularly attend Catholic mass, I may find a respite at church on a weekday morning after mass where I can sit in a pew, close my eyes and just breathe.

Generally, there isn't a right or wrong place to meditate. It's wherever you feel comfortable and at peace.

Why:

This entire book is dedicated to why a yoga and meditation practice has numerous benefits. The key to achieving happiness, peace, love of self and health is to remain consistent, especially as you heal from a broken heart. And it's just as important to continue practicing regularly long after you've recovered.

Chapter 13:
Search & Rescue,
Search & Recovery

It's human nature to constantly seek happiness as well as the answer to the question: Who am I?

I know that the times when I'm happy, whether I'm in a relationship or not, I think to myself, I couldn't be happier or I like where I'm at right now. During happy times, my desire to better myself, ironically, remains dormant.

So when tragedy strikes in the form of a heart-wrenching breakup, my mind, body, and spirit all fall into self-help mode. Sure, it's perfectly fine to ask for help, support, advice and a lending ear from family and friends but in times of personal turmoil, you also have to help yourself.

I believe we're all constantly seeking in this life and for some of us we're only inclined to set out on a journey to find ourselves when we're troubled. This is the universe's way of telling us "Your pain is your opportunity to learn, to heal, and to grow."

To my fellow broken-hearted brethren I say, "Be your own White Knight. Don't rely on your family, your friends and most certainly not on a new lover to rescue you. Save yourself."

Often times, we wish for another person to come into our lives to love us, help us get over our ex and the heartache. It's not the wisest thing to do. If you're like me, it takes a long time to get over someone you really loved. You owe it to yourself to take time to get to know yourself again.

Yoga and meditation cannot only navigate you on your travels toward the path to self-discovery, but they can be your lifesavers as well. As I recover, I'm getting to know my body again, appreciating what it can do through the various asanas or yoga poses. Through deep breathing and meditation, I marvel at where my mind can take me. With my mind, I can go back to the past and revisit good and bad memories. As memorable as some nice memories are, I'd rather stay in the present. The mind can take you where you want to go and hopefully, through meditation, it will lead you on the road to recovery.

While the word "recovery" may, for some, evoke references to certain types of addiction, I use the word "recovery" because I believe that when we're trying to heal from heartbreak, we are, in a sense, recovering from an addiction to our former lovers from whom we may have once depended on as a source of happiness. Now, we're working on depending on ourselves—our thoughts and our actions—to create our happiness. This, for me, is where recovery takes place. It is, in essence, a return to self.

So keep searching for answers about life. Curiosity seekers may tend to frequent Zen centers, self-improvement workshops, support groups, or take art classes. Then there's always my best friends—my books.

I'm accumulating an extensive yoga and meditation
library as we speak and so can you, if you're so inclined.
Remember: when you're in a bind, still your mind.

Chapter 14:
Getting Through
Weekend & Holiday Blues

Ah, weekends. You keep your mind preoccupied from Monday to Friday with work, school, your family, spending time with friends and before you know it, it's the dreaded weekend again.

When I was juggling fulltime newspaper reporting and grad school—and demanding deadlines for both—I looked forward to weekends. Even though at the time my ex and I spent time together during the week, weekends meant exploring the hidden treasures of the Bay Area or hanging out with friends. In other words, weekends were for cultivating quality couple time.

Post-breakup weekends have been the worst. I get all antsy on Fridays trying to feverishly fill my weekends with activities so there's absolutely no time to think about my ex and miss all those wonderful weekends we spent together. Then I realize that the key to post-breakup weekend survival and happiness is—drum roll, please—being in the moment.

Even as I write this, I'm still learning (did I mention that living in the present is an ongoing lesson until you get it right?) how not to try to be so controlling and to just surrender to what may come. After all, a meticulously planned weekend jam-packed with activities doesn't guarantee happiness.

Be open, receptive, spontaneous, and responsive to all possibilities with no expectations. Recently, I've been trying (it's been hard, but I deserve at least an A for effort!) to allow the weekend to just be. I'm not saying don't make plans. Just embrace the unexpected and try not to get all worked up because you don't have plans.

Instead, use the weekend to enjoy your own company, take yourself on a date, and take yourself out for lunch or to a matinee or to the gallery or museum. Call up a friend you haven't chatted with for a while. Ditch the Internet or TV for a day (it can be liberating to take a break from technology!) and instead write a letter to a faraway friend or read a good book at a park.

And, of course, there's always yoga and meditation. If you're bothered by crowded yoga classes on weekends overflowing with people who don't practice during the week because of work (if you're one of those busy people, try to make some time to fit yoga into your weekday schedule. It's a worthy investment of your time especially during a hectic week), then practice on your own. You already know yoga and meditation are portable practices.

Try meditation outdoors during sunrise or sunset. You don't have to have a lot of money or go anywhere exotic to take advantage of a yoga retreat. Create your own. Simply attend a yoga or meditation class or both held on a weekend, then treat yourself to a "spa" salad lunch or dinner, and then write about your experience in your journal.

Post-breakup holidays can also be a drag, but only if you let them be. Try to approach weekends and holidays, including your birthday, with a different perspective. Declare to yourself: "Now I can finally spend weekends and holidays the way I want to!"

My ex hated the commercialism of Christmas and Valentine's Day and, frankly, I couldn't agree more. However, while I disliked the material and consumerist aspect of those occasions, I embraced the tradition of getting together with family during the holidays and enjoying a romantic dinner with my boyfriend on Valentine's Day. I believe Christmas and the spirit of giving and Valentine's Day and the spirit of loving should take place every day.

Still, holidays spent nursing a broken heart can be challenging. While you can't erase the pain, at least, strive to count your blessings. Instead of agonizing over "happier" holidays when you were coupled, think about the different ways you can spend the holidays now. Come up with exciting, new ways to celebrate. You can be happy again. I'm already thinking about ringing in the New Year practicing yoga and meditation somewhere, maybe by myself if classes aren't available.

Valentine's Day shouldn't be the only day you give yourself some love (I think you already know that, right?). But if you insist on celebrating Valentine's Day and assert you can do so alone or with girlfriends, then by all means, do so. Since spas tend to get busy on the day itself, book a massage, facial or a hair appointment the day before or after Valentine's Day. Better yet, buy yourself some flowers. Years ago, my good friend Stephanie got me into buying flowers for myself as she would do for herself at a local Farmers Market as a pick-me-up treat.

And, do I have to tell you that the best way to beat birthday and Valentine's Day blues is through yoga and meditation practice? This year, I started my birthday morning off with an at-home yoga session. It was one of the best gifts I've ever given myself.

Celebrate life. Celebrate you.

ॐ

Chapter 15:
Creating Your Own
Power Spots

As creatures of habit, we tend to get attached to favorite spots anywhere we go—a seat in front of a class, a seat in the center of a movie theater six rows up, a favorite booth in a restaurant. You get the picture.

The danger of getting too attached to certain things, places and people (ahem, let go of that ex already!) is that when you don't get what you're used to, all hell breaks loose. Or so you think.

It doesn't have to be that way. Practice getting used to the concepts of impermanence (more on this later) and nonattachment. The more accustomed you are to the fact that nothing stays the same, the better off you'll be.

You can start living this concept in an empowering way by choosing different spots inside and outside your home for you to meditate or create. Some people call them sacred spaces. I call them "power spots."

I first heard this term used a few years ago when I broke my right foot in a bike accident. My boyfriend at the time met his friends at a property his friends had just purchased up in the hills of Benicia, a small suburban city north of the San Francisco Bay. Since that hill was perched on what was believed to be sacred Native American ground, we started to meditate and ask the Universe for things we wanted.

I asked for my foot to heal, for work conditions to improve, for inspiration to write a novel and to get into graduate school. Within six months, my foot was healed, I got transferred back to my old office to work with my awesome former editor, I wrote the first draft of a novel and I got accepted into the Master of Fine Arts in Creative Writing program at Mills College. How's that for a power spot?

Since that hill was private property, I couldn't get too attached to that spot even though I felt so empowered there. So I had to have a few other places where I could manifest my goals.

One place is actually called "The Spot," a neighborhood café in Pleasant Hill where I wrote several grad school papers, hold creative writing workshops and where I've been writing chapters of this book. The friendly owners make my reading and writing experiences there worthwhile.

My most powerful spot to date has been "Yoga Lake" where I do standing yoga poses near a lake at Hidden Lakes Park in Martinez, a nice pit stop during my trail walking. I try to go there at least twice a week to do yoga. There's nothing like practicing yoga outdoors where you literally feel grounded and connected to the earth.

Another one of my favorite power spots is the gazebo on the grounds of Buddha Gate Monastery where I meditate for at least half an hour or so.

You can create sacred space at home perhaps a corner of a room with pillows, a blanket and candles to light as you meditate, pray, practice yoga or write in your journal.

A power spot is wherever you feel the most at peace to create works of art and various projects. It's a place where you can send out your dreams and make your intentions known to the Universe and know that with hard work, determination and trust, the Universe will respond in kind.

Chapter 16:
Warding Off Negative Energy, Thoughts & Actions

On the path toward recovery, you're going to be plagued with negative thoughts, reenacting the breakup scene in your mind, and worrying about what might happen if you run into your ex.

If you don't have a choice and still have contact with your ex because you share custody of your children or you have to work together, it's even more difficult to get your ex out of sight and out of mind despite your best efforts.

You need to make the choice to not let her or him invade your thoughts any longer. Remember when you were still together and you valued the need for personal space between the two of you because it was healthy? Well, now that you're no longer a couple these physical and inner spaces are even more important. Believe it or not, there are people, myself included, who consciously choose to keep their exes in their lives against the advice of loved ones and their own conscience. What are we hanging on to?

A good friend Sara likened someone breaking your heart to someone taking a knife and cutting your finger off. No matter how you slice it, she said, (no pun intended), it's still pain. Would you go back to someone after they've cut your finger? Why would you still welcome the person who practically drove a stake through your heart? If someone told you there was a room filled with gold coins but that the room was also infused with poisonous fumes, would you still want to go inside?

We all know that when it comes to the heart, there is no rhyme or reason. We don't often think about what's best for us in the long run. All we want is for things to be the way they once were. This state of living in the past is so detrimental to us that we don't even realize it. We think, how can reminiscing about happy memories with our ex be so damaging? They are, we reason, happy, not sad, memories, after all.

Even remembering the good times can bring sadness and an intense longing for what was and what can no longer be. For those of you thinking "Oh, well, we're going through a rough patch right now. We both need to find ourselves first before we find each other again," I say—forget it. I'm not saying don't give up on love. You deserve to be loved by someone who will love and cherish you unconditionally. Don't waste your time wondering whether you and your ex will get back together. If your love was meant to be, only time will tell. In the meantime, don't get your hopes up.

All I'm emphasizing is to stay focused on the task at hand—loving and healing yourself first. So before you get the impulse to pick up the phone and dial your ex's number, stop and think. Have you dialed up your own number lately and checked in with yourself first?

Meditation and yoga has taught me a very important lesson in self control. For the most part, the yoga postures are slow and deliberate so that you become accustomed to checking in with yourself to make sure your body is moving at a comfortable pace and that the posture isn't uncomfortable. As you monitor your positions, you listen to your own breath before you venture into any sort of compromising movement or pose. You are practicing the art of self control and awareness. You wouldn't knowingly do anything to deliberately hurt yourself, would you? Then why would you call your ex and get your heart broken again?

Apply the same principle with your thoughts. While we can't stop negative thoughts from coming, we don't have to empower them. Acknowledge that the negative thought is there then choose to think about something else. Better yet, do something positive—call a friend, take a walk, watch a funny movie—anything to get your mind off that negative thought.

One of the affirmation cards from Louise L. Hay's Power Thought Cards, reads, "It's only a thought, and a thought can be changed. I am not limited by any past thinking. I choose my thoughts with care. I constantly have new insights and new ways of looking at my world. I am willing to change and grow."

Visualization through meditation can help ensure your mind isn't constantly enslaved with negativity. Mentally picture yourself moving on, taking a trip, or better yet, book yourself a trip if you can afford it. This may be your time to actually go to a place you've only dreamed about. Today, it can be your reality.

In June, just four months after the breakup, I hopped on a plane to Rome with a perfect stranger. Well, he was actually a co-worker of a close friend of mine who worked for United Airlines. Over the years,

I'd traveled with Eloi to various places like Milan, Philippines, and Las Vegas courtesy of her "Buddy Pass," and this was supposed to be one of those trips. Instead, Eloi and her hubby, Ron, got sick and I had to travel with Bon, Eloi's co-worker.

Let me tell you up front. It was a strictly platonic, non-romantically-oriented trip. I may have been visiting Rome, one of the most romantic places on Earth, but romance wasn't predominantly on my mind. Of course, I couldn't help but feel a bit of longing for my ex as I watched other couples holding hands or embracing while exploring one of the great wonders of the world, the Roman Coliseum. As I stood in the summer heat looking at the massive pillars that dated back thousands of years, I couldn't help but realize that this gargantuan structure existed long before my problems occurred and will continue to exist long after. The important thing to realize was that I was here—now—I kept reminding myself. There will never be another moment quite like this one as feelings and experiences do change from moment to moment.

Then, it occurred to me, that the last time my heart was broken a few years ago, I fled. That was how I dealt with the negativity that infused within me. I escaped to Spain for a summer to take up an intensive Spanish language course at the Complutense Universidad de Madrid, followed by a short trip to Paris at the end of the six-week program. I wanted to get as far away from the heartbreak as possible.

But then, I figured out, it didn't matter how far I traveled—the heartbreak and emotions that came along with it traveled with me. That didn't mean I couldn't have a good time. I was in Spain, after all, living it up, drinking sangria, watching flamenco performances, taking flamenco dance lessons, frequenting tapas bars and enjoying churros con chocolate at a chocolateria at 2 a.m. in the middle of the week with just hours to spare before I headed off to a grueling four hours of Spanish classes at the university the next morning.

The highlight of my trip didn't occur until I reached Paris, however. It may have been at the tail end of my trip but my spiritual journey was just getting started. It was at the roof of the Notre Dame Cathedral, with the fascinating grotesque gargoyles alongside me, that my creative soul started to open up and all this literary blood that lay dormant for years under my objective, journalistic writing skin came pouring forth unabashedly. So, I surrendered to it. I turned to poetry to find my literary voice again. The language of poetry helped my embattled soul find peace after despair.

Back to my recent trip to Rome. Since I turned my trip to Spain and France as a healing journey rather than an escape, the last thing I wanted was to use Rome as a way to forget my heartbreak. So, I was present at every moment—present at the Roman Coliseum, present at St. Peter's Basilica at the Vatican, present as I marveled at the celestial ceiling splashed with the timeless art of Michelangelo. As I was present in my surroundings, I was also present with whatever I was feeling—joy, sadness, longing, admiration, peace. There was a certain ethereal feeling of experiencing heartache in the midst of so much beauty. I felt I was truly living a fully dimensional life—breathing in light, breathing out darkness, breathing in beauty, breathing out despair.

The beauty of art and the beast that was my heartache, the positive and the negative, the good and bad memories—all existed in some synergistic way for me to realize that to truly live and learn the lessons of life, it can't all be good, and it can't all be bad. Living a one-dimensional life wasn't living at all. The unplanned trip to Rome, no matter how whirlwind it was, wasn't me escaping my problems. It was simply me punctuating my life with adventure. It was in daring myself to do what I thought I didn't have time or the courage for that I learned what else I could attain if I only allowed myself to do it.

So visualize yourself doing something you've always wanted to do. This thought process gets the wheels set in motion for actual doing rather than just thinking, but there's nothing wrong with a virtual tour around the world or a good, old fashioned armchair travel through an awesome book.

To combat negative thoughts, it also helps to make a list of your accomplishments no matter how small. It's the little, simple things that can bring us the greatest pleasure.

I can't emphasize enough the power of positive affirmations. My first taste of conditioning my mind to think positively through affirmations was through a little book called *Inner Wisdom*, by Louise L. Hay. It helped me get through heartbreak from a brief but intense romance I experienced six years ago. And now, I've had my heart broken again, this time much more excruciating. We tend to repeat our past hurts until we learn our lessons.

Heartbreak is a part of life. Even though it hurts like hell, we do learn from our pain and will be better equipped to handle any trials that come our way.

Positive affirmations help to root yourself in thoughts and actions that keep you feeling good. You need to do more than just say them—you need to believe them. As you meditate or go about your day, weave those affirmations into the core of your being.

Chapter 17:
The Gift of a Furry Friend

I am a firm believer that nothing and no one can place us firmly in the present more than a beloved animal companion or furry family member.

Sure, children may anchor you in the present with their adorable antics, their various demands, needs and growing pains. Although I've never been a mother of human children, I've heard from close friends that having a child can be the most gratifying experience in the world. As you're healing from your heartbreak, your child can be your saving grace as you focus your attention on the blessings of parenthood and the miracle of life you brought into the world.

But for those of us without children, our pets are our children. Since yoga's benefits extend beyond the mat, having an animal grace your life with its presence is a great way to practice Karma Yoga. There is something spiritual about having an animal bless your life whether the animal is your pet or not.

I've always had cats in my life growing up either as pets or strays our family took care of but I was also blessed with the role of foster parent to litters from the shelter. Being a foster parent to shelter animals is one of the noblest roles a person can take on in life because you're basically saving lives by taking care of baby cats not quite ready for adoption. Kittens under the care of foster parents get the nourishment, socialization, and love they need. Sadly, hundreds, thousands of cats who are deemed ineligible for adoption are euthanized. This is reality. So this is where animal foster parenting comes in—you give these animals a chance to live.

My ex and I took on foster kitten parenting two years ago when we cared for our first litter. While we embraced our roles as foster kitten parents, sadly, four out of the five kittens we fostered had to be euthanized because of various ailments. Only one survived—Domino—a beautiful male tuxedo kitten that became the love of my life. Since I'd lost four kittens to illness, I was determined to do whatever I could to ensure Domino's survival. Eventually and thankfully the kitten thrived and ultimately got adopted. It was bittersweet.

While the goal of foster parenting is adoption, I formed an unbreakable, unshakeable bond with Domino—he was my child. I'd never loved an animal as much as I loved Domino. So, naturally I was crushed when he left. Still, I was grateful he survived despite the odds and he found a wonderful new home. Linda, the woman who adopted him, has been a great mom to Domino. She's been good about keeping me posted on his progress and he's grown up to be a beautiful big boy.

The following year, my ex and I fostered several more litters and, I'm happy to report, all kittens stayed healthy and got adopted. But the spring before the next wave of kittens ever reached our care, my ex broke up with me. Since then, I've been helping my sister socialize shelter cats and kittens at Petsmart in Richmond, a role I've come to embrace as passionately as foster parenting.

The experience of socializing, feeding and playing with these cats has been extremely rewarding. However, as with the case in foster parenting, it's easy to fall in love with the animals. Because I get so attached, I often worry about them—will they get adopted by people who will truly care for them? Will they get adopted at all? What happens if and when they return to the shelter?

This whole experience has taught me a lot about detachment, impermanence, how short life is, how we often take it for granted, how nothing stays the same, and how nothing lasts forever. For instance, each time I worried how the kittens would fare once they left our care I realized all I could do was care for them the best way I could, then release them. The same is true for the kittens and cats I socialized at Petsmart. I've come to accept the fact that I can't save them all—all I can do is love them and wish them well wherever they may go. I try to apply this same principle with my ex. I loved him in the best way I could, but I can't control his actions and the course his life will take.

Animals have taught me important lessons about nonattachment. It's hard not to get attached to our furry little friends. A friend once commented that to get attached to animals was a "good attachment" as opposed to a "bad attachment" to your ex. Still, any type of attachment as well as any unwillingness to accept that nothing stays the same hinders your path to happiness.

In the meantime, as you go through your heartache, consider spending time with animals—your own pet, your friends' pets, or volunteer with your local shelter or rescue group. Better yet, adopt a shelter animal or lend your time as a foster parent and help save some lives.

As you hold adorable, furry creatures in your arms, you know that the animals won't judge you and will love you unconditionally as they look up at you with eyes full of gratitude. This is the practice of Karma Yoga at its finest.

ॐ

Chapter 18:
Nothing Lasts Forever

Whenever you read or hear someone say, "Everything changes. Nothing lasts forever," your first impulse immediately after a painful breakup may be to curl up in the nearest corner and cry.

"Why didn't our love last? Isn't real love supposed to last? After all, I tried so hard to be the perfect girlfriend (or boyfriend). I loved with all my heart. That will never change."

That's exactly what I thought—that true love lasts forever. And you know what? It does. If you truly loved the person you invested your time with, the love you have for that person doesn't have to end even though your former mate has stopped loving you or doesn't want to be with you. I can't emphasize this enough— you can't teach the heart to stop loving.

But you can train your mind to embrace the concept of impermanence. I can't tell you how often I either heard or read the saying "The only thing constant is change," and initially this made me sick to my stomach. Like many people dealing with heartbreak, I was in denial that the relationship was over. How could my ex switch the off button just like that?

While it hasn't been easy, thinking that change is inevitable helps to ease the pain of a breakup. You start to think that change is a constant—people, feelings, thoughts, jobs, preferences, values—they all change. Even the whole world changes and it's up to us to adapt to the changes in order to survive.

Consider this: even if you do find true love again and it lasts fifty years, the fact is someone is going to die—you'll both die eventually. There's no way around death—it's a part of life. For our emotional survival, we need to accept that nothing lasts forever. We can't expect things, situations, and circumstances to stay the same.

So rather than mope as we dwell on this, we should feel elated. We may be in tremendous pain right now but this pain, just like the joy we experienced in our relationship, won't last forever. Thankfully, it will pass.

Does this mean we can't ever be happy for a long while? Happiness is a state we put ourselves in. Many spiritual philosophers claim that we are inherently happy—that happiness is our birthright. So when we're suffering, it is our job to put ourselves back into our natural, happy state. We create our own happiness, remember?

When I think of impermanence, I think of all the kittens I've fostered. I can't keep them forever. They either got adopted or died of illness. Even if I did keep them, cats eventually die, even if they do have nine lives. I like to think that we shared a genuine bond during the time I cared for them and that love will never end. In fact, I still think about those kittens to this day. But I know there will be many other cats whose presence will grace my life.

How does impermanence relate to yoga and meditation? Just as our exes can change their minds about us, our experiences on the mat can change. If we are successful in doing balancing poses one day, we may not succeed the next. We may be able to sit through a half hour of thought-free meditation one night (experienced practitioners, I'm told, can achieve this), but struggle to ward off negative thoughts creeping upon us the following night.

Don't worry if your sadness doesn't seem to go away or if you seem to be making emotional progress one day but feel sad the next. It's not a setback. Tell yourself that it's all part of the grieving process. Keep meditating. Meditating makes us aware that we need to accept that all of life is a series of ups and downs whether we are in the midst of broken heartedness or not.

Meditate on the fact that, in life, nothing stays the same. The sooner you embrace this principle, the better your chance of gaining inner peace.

Don't force yourself to stop loving the person who hurt you. You may continue loving her or him or you may not. Only time will tell you when it's time to stop or continue loving. Listen to your heart. What is it telling you?

In the meantime, you can continue to love someone from a distance. Just as the pain will one day pass, so may the love. The only love that will remain is the truest, purest love—the kind of love that emanates from one who has genuinely mastered the art of loving oneself.

Chapter 19:
Do Unto Others

While recovering from a breakup, one may become anti-social, a hermit of sorts. People cope with heartbreak in different ways. Some want to be around people all the time, while others want to be left alone.

Strive to strike a balance between quality alone time and spending time with family and friends. Reaching out to others in need may be a good way to put your own problems in perspective. Simply hanging out with friends can remind you how precious life can be.

Time spent helping family, friends and even strangers is an extension of practicing Karma Yoga. Giving in this case is more than a charitable act. You're giving of yourself and all the goodness in you without expecting anything in return. When someone you love has hurt you, there's a tendency to think the world owes you. You may think, "Why should I do anything for anyone? After all, I'm the one who's hurting. I give and keep giving and all I get is rejection."

Treating others with kindness is a great antidote to combating the hurt the breakup caused and the damage that was done to your spirit. Karma is the

Golden Rule in effect and you want to continue spreading that karma all around.

Start spreading good karma with your loved ones. Take your parents out to dinner, take your nieces and nephews (or children, if you have them) to the movies or visit a sick friend.

Giving isn't always monetary. You can donate your time to local nonprofit organizations supporting such causes as the food bank, adult literacy, homeless shelters, soup kitchens, animal shelters, and animal rescue groups. Other than visiting the felines at Petsmart, I often spend time socializing kittens and cats previously at the shelter's 'Death Row' who have been rescued by dedicated volunteers.

Whether I'm with these felines or with people in need, I forget my own troubles. I'm not saying that by helping others you're giving your own problems less importance. Remember, no problem is too small. It's just that when you're thinking about others besides yourself you're recognizing that we're all connected in this world. When you give, you're not only healing yourself, you're helping to heal the world one cause, one animal, one person at a time.

As you reach out, remain calm. Don't walk around as if you're holding the world's problems and your own on your shoulders. Yes, you can vent your anger and frustrations but by immersing yourself in your causes, you are channeling your hurt in a positive way.

It's important as you heal to not get impatient or irritated with the people around you. Don't take your anger out on them. Let them know what you are going through. Treat strangers equally with kindness. Know that pain is a part of life. Everybody hurts. Reaching out to others will help you see that.

Don't worry if spending too much time helping others takes you away from yoga classes. Christy Turlington-Burns, model, activist, yogi and author of *Living Yoga,* the first book that enlightened me about the spiritual aspects of yoga, sums up this principle best in an interview in the Vogue magazine August 2009 issue in which she talked about juggling graduate school, family and activism.

"I miss yoga, but yoga is much more than the physical postures," Christy says. "I believe what I am doing now is the most important yoga, which is service. Service is a fundamental part of being human. It's a potential that needs to be cultivated. People are always so concerned with what they might lose."

Learn to give back quietly without recognition. It's not important to announce your generosity to the whole world. You know you're giving back and that's enough. Your opinion of yourself is the one that matters. So pat yourself on the back.

There's nothing wrong with giving back to yourself first. You've heard people say to pay yourself first by saving money in the bank. Giving yourself the gift of yoga as you spread good karma to others is a huge way of investing in yourself.

Part Three

Keeping It Real:
Now, the Future & Beyond

The beauty of life is, while we cannot undo what is done, we can see it, understand it, learn from it, and change. So that every new moment is spent not in regret, guilt, fear or anger, but in wisdom, understanding and love.

—Jennifer Edwards

Chapter 20:
The Three R's

Remove the word expectation from your vocabulary. Don't expect to be over your ex by a certain time. You can't expect to go through a typical grieving process. There is no such thing. While healing your broken heart, it's important to heed the three R's:

RECOGNIZE that there isn't a normal way of grieving. Everyone grieves differently. Forget what you heard about the typical stages of the grieving process—shock, denial, anger, depression, understanding and acceptance. Getting over someone and healing can't be rushed. There is no such thing as an express path to healing. If you wish for the pain to go away soon, you may be missing out on a golden opportunity to grow and learn from your ordeal. This doesn't mean you are continuing to torture yourself. It just means that as you take care of yourself you are paying attention to the lessons life is teaching you.

Don't be pressured by people who may say "It's been a year already—get over it!" Remind yourself that in this process, you're doing more than just getting over your ex—you're healing yourself. That takes time.

Be RESPONSIVE to the lessons your experience is teaching you. Don't resist the pain. Resisting will only create more suffering. Your pain is reaching out to you, calling you and you need to respond by being mindful to every emotion that's coming your way. You can't will your way out of pain. The only way to get through this and emerge as a survivor full of wisdom and enlightenment is by letting the pain run its course.

There's no magic pill created for you to wish pain away. Listen to fear, anger, and anguish and find out the root cause of why it hurts so much. It's obvious you're hurting because your ex broke your heart but after some time has passed and you're still in pain, ask yourself why. What can you let go of or take up to make the process more beneficial?

Be RECEPTIVE to all possibilities and opportunities. Since you can't take the fast track to recovery, just sit still and take the scenic route. This means that as you heal, there may be a few "setbacks" along the way. You could be in denial for a very long time. You can be angry for just as long. You could be fine one day and depressed the next. But stay open to the possibility that these so called "setbacks" could be signs that you still need to work on a few things. If you've been paying attention, then you would know what these issues are.

For instance, just when I thought I could go for hours without thinking about my ex, I'd have predominant thoughts of him so that it was hard to think of anything else. Random things would trigger random memories—good and bad. A recent full moon took me back to the time my ex and I walked a labyrinth for the first time one September evening accompanied by the woman he eventually hooked up with after breaking up with me. As I write this, I also just now experienced a flashback of the time when I had just arrived from Paris and my ex surprised me with a bouquet of roses and airport pickup.

Whenever bad feelings arise, I simply allow the feeling or memory to play itself out and remind myself I'm not there anymore. I am here in the present. I use the same technique for a fond memory. I tell myself I will feel that good again with time and patience. Allow your breath to guide you back here from the past—give yourself the gift of breath to stay rooted in the present. Our breath is a beautiful reminder that we have survived our turbulent past. Each breath we take invites us to appreciate the present, which is indeed a Present—a Gift given to us in the Highest Order.

Chapter 21:
Beginner's Mind

It's so easy to get a bit cocky or overconfident when you've been practicing yoga for quite awhile. Yoga isn't about achieving a certain status or level.

If certain classes are categorized as beginner or advanced or labeled as levels one, two or three, they are usually used to help you gauge your comfort level from a physical standpoint.

But even experienced yogis as well as instructors have their off days. You may be super flexible one day and very tight the next. You may have balance issues one week and discover you're as steady and focused as can be the following week.

The key thing to remember is, in yoga as in the rest of life, no day is ever the same. Your body changes just as your mood changes. You also need to keep your ego in check. Suppose you just received a promotion at work. There's no guarantee your status will stay the same. You could face a demotion or job elimination. That's the reality—the impermanence of life.

As hard as it may be for you to do so right now, just think back for a second of the happiest time you ever spent with your ex. Remember how madly in love you were? The passion you shared? Did you ever find yourself wishing time would stand still as you and your lover watched an amazing sunset by the ocean? Did you hope the happy times would never end?

Impermanence doesn't have to be a harsh reality. Joy as well as pain doesn't last forever. We can learn humility from our experience. Being humble keeps us from approaching life with high expectations that only set us up for disappointment. This doesn't mean we can't have standards. We just have to stay grounded in reality and learn to take things in stride.

Yoga teaches us to stay humble—to always approach life with a beginner's mind. Doing so will keep our minds and hearts open to experiencing new things. Even things we've tried before become new experiences again. This is how to continue practicing yoga with passion so that the practice itself and your attitude towards yoga never get old.

Approach each yoga session with newfound energy by simply acknowledging the blessing of a chance to start the day off on a clean slate.

Try to apply the same attitude with other aspects of your life. The commute to work, for instance, doesn't have to be a routine. If you drive, try taking public transportation, carpool with a co-worker or friend or bike to work. New and different experiences keep you on your toes, challenge you and help you to not take things for granted. Finding new ways to do things gives you a fresh perspective.

In matters of the heart it's easy to approach a new relationship with caution and trepidation. You fear getting rejected again. But it's a risk you take when you give your heart to another. Still, try not to enter into a new relationship with a jaded outlook on love. Being in the present means you're willing to start anew despite past heartaches.

Hopefully, you've taken some time to work on yourself before plunging into the next relationship. If you haven't devoted ample time to heal yourself first, you're not likely to find happiness in the next relationship. Remember that recovering from heartbreak means more than just getting over the person who broke your heart. It means making yourself happy first without the aid of another lover.

The 'forever new' concept applies on as well as off the mat. If you feel you may be in a rut by attending the same yoga class, it may be your outlook. Change your attitude and your experience may change. You can always try new teachers, new classes or new styles to keep the passion in your practice. But keep in mind, whichever road you take, no one can create that inner glow, that inner spark, that renewed sense of purpose and passion, but you.

Chapter 22:
In Someone Else's Shoes

In Bliss Wood's moving book *Empowering Your Life With Yoga*, she beautifully states that, "When we can sense from within ourselves what it must be like to experience someone else's situation, then we have found compassion."

For me, compassion is simply being able to put yourself in another's shoes. When my ex broke up with me, I couldn't imagine that he was conscious of how he was hurting me as he delivered his breakup speech in the most cold-hearted way, hurling his hurtful words as though he was throwing darts in my direction, piercing me relentlessly in the heart. He placed the blame solely on me, faulting me for my inability to make him happy. He never took accountability for his own actions.

My ex further pulverized my heart six weeks later by admitting to pursuing a relationship with the woman he insisted he didn't have feelings for—the woman whom he chastised me for worrying about. I remember the day we spoke on the phone after I found out about the two of them.

"Do you know what it feels like when someone you love loves someone else?" I asked him.

"Yes, I do know," he replied.

"I would only hope that you would have some compassion for what I'm going through," I said.

"I do. I have compassion," he insisted.

Truthfully, I didn't exactly feel compassion oozing from his voice. Nor did I sense compassion was pouring from his heart. I could be wrong, but how could he possibly feel what I was going through at that moment when he obviously had moved on? At that moment, he was bathed in the euphoric state of a new romance—that was all he seemed to be concerned about.

I think back about my ex-boyfriend from fifteen years ago. Although we worked together and got along okay, we were not each other's soul mates—that was clear from the start. But my inexperience with relationships coupled with my need to give into peer pressure (all my friends had boyfriends or were engaged) inevitably resulted in the demise of the relationship. He called it quits—mainly because he had moved back to Oregon—citing "we were better served as friends," as he wrote in his breakup letter.

Rejection in any form is never easy but I wasn't exactly crushed. I initially tagged him as the bad guy but he later revealed a redeeming quality about himself. He sent a letter to me months after the breakup to find out how I was doing. By then, I was over him. Still, the compassion he showed in his letter moved me. He took the time to inquire about my well being because he wrote to say he was concerned about how I dealt with the breakup.

Needless to say, I really wasn't too broken up about the relationship because I eventually realized I deserved better and that we really weren't meant to be together. But the fact that he reached out to apologize showed his sense of compassion. By getting in touch with me several months after breaking up with me, he took a huge risk that I wouldn't acknowledge him because he thought I would still be angry and hurt. But his willingness to ensure my well being meant more to him than a bruised ego. That's compassion.

When my recent ex broke up with me, he tried back peddling a bit by calling me to find out how I was doing, but I realized it was more for his benefit than mine. I felt he couldn't have cared less how I felt otherwise he wouldn't have said the things he said in the callous way he did.

What's shocking to me was his blatant admission of issues I was unaware of. He expressed concerns to me I never even knew he had. Weren't couples who cared about each other supposed to communicate? If something was bothering him, wasn't he supposed to express that concern with me first so we could at least talk about it and work our way through it?

As far as I was concerned, I didn't commit a heinous crime. I didn't have an affair or even accuse him of having one. He claimed I didn't show enough interest in his work and that I hadn't been working hard enough. "You've been on thin ice for awhile now," was his remark.

While a few days post breakup he expressed how sorry he was, he then proceeded to criticize me some more to a point where I wondered, "Why am I even here listening to this?" What was the point of his apology? Still, I listened to his concerns and only his since he didn't even give me a chance to tell my side.

Perhaps to redeem himself for his vile behavior, my ex reiterated that while he was "done with the

relationship, you can come and go as you please." So, I
foolishly took him up on that offer—still going over to
his place, still going out to dinner with him, still going
grocery shopping with him. We even took a Power
Point class we had signed up for pre-breakup, but that
neither one of us wanted to drop. It was almost as
though we hadn't broken up. I was still in denial the
relationship was over.

But one evening as we were having dinner when
he casually referred to me as a friend, I felt sick to my
stomach—it hit me just where I stood in the
relationship, he made that quite clear. How could I go
from being a girlfriend to being a friend in a blink of an
eye and turn the switch from on to off just like that?
How could he be so nonchalant?

Friends told me he didn't deserve to be my
friend—that my friendship had to be earned and frankly,
they were right. He didn't deserve my friendship. But
did I listen? Initially, no. We continued to hang out as
"friends" until I kept hearing him mention that woman
and I discovered in his refrigerator the leftover food she
prepared for him for a previous dinner at her place.

It wasn't until that fateful day—my dad's
birthday—when I called him and he was up at Lake
Tahoe skiing with a friend that I found out the woman
was also with him.

"Is she your girlfriend?" I asked, a chill climbing
up my spine.

"It's sort of headed in that direction," he replied,
driving a stake through my heart.

It was then that I knew I had to detach myself
from him. How could someone you love replace you
within six weeks? How could I still associate with him
knowing he had given his heart to someone else? I've

heard of former lovers who remained friends but I couldn't stay in contact with him, be his friend, for my sake. For one thing, I still loved the guy and I still wasn't over him. I had to do more than just get over him—I had to heal myself.

One time, as my ex and I went grocery shopping post breakup, I commented on how our friend had yet to get over his breakup with his ex, another friend of ours.

"Sometimes people take a long time to get over someone," I said, thinking about myself.

"Not everyone takes that long," my ex commented, probably referring to his own self.

Who's to say what the future will hold? It's possible our paths may cross again. In the meantime, I'm learning what it takes to practice compassion in my own life. If my relationship with my ex had to end, then it had to end. I accept that. What I wish, not just for myself, but for my ex and the world is that we, as people and as inhabitants of this planet, practice compassion, which starts with ourselves.

We do not wish to inflict suffering on ourselves, so why should we do it to others? When we are faced with ending a relationship with another person because it is for the best interest of both parties, then can we commit to doing so in a respectful manner, in a way that helps rather than harms another person?

Whenever I act or speak about something I may not be in agreement with or if I must voice my opinion or frustration about such things as customer dissatisfaction, I usually do so with tact. We need to be mindful of the fact that while we would like to set things right in our world, we must consider the other being who is also trying to make their way through this worldly existence. The waiter at a restaurant or bridge toll taker could have had a bad day and didn't mean to take her or his frustrations out on you.

By the same token, if you've had a bad day or a relatively unhappy life, the problem is with you and not with the other person. Do not take out your issues on someone else. Have some compassion. Try to feel what it's like to be in their shoes.

Whether or not you have experienced what the other person has experienced, make it a point to be there for that person. You may not know what it feels like to lose a parent, or a spouse to divorce, but have some empathy. You may not think the type of loss your friend is going through is a big deal, but when you put yourself in your friend's place, you'll see how much this person is hurting. You could be hurting in the same way over some other issue. Everyone grieves differently, but by showing support for your friend, your loved one or for a stranger, you are practicing yoga in one of the best ways off the mat.

You are reaching out to others and thus reaching out to yourself with the love you have within you. You are practicing compassion—one of the greatest gifts you give to another person, an animal, the planet and yourself.

Chapter 23:
Compassion & Beyond

At some point in the process of healing you're going to face the prospect of forgiveness, which doesn't come instantly. It takes time to forgive. That said, my intention is not to preach about forgiveness but rather to help you, as I help myself, see ways we can advance toward that state and hope that we may one day attain it. Forgiveness is the key that sets us free.

When I think about the tale of a woman scorned, my friend's aunt comes to mind. My friend told me her aunt's husband left her for another woman and thirty years later, her aunt is still bitter.

"I don't want to end up like my aunt," said my friend whose own marriage was in peril.

"Me neither," I agreed.

We go into and come out of a painful, but growing experience to be better, not bitter people. So, as I think about what it means to have compassion in my own experience, I try to put myself in my ex's shoes.

While I believe he could have ended the relationship in a more communicative, more compassionate manner, I take some accountability for the way things ended. While I tried to be this perfect girlfriend—I cooked healthy vegetarian meals, watched his cats and his house as he took trips abroad, as he went skiing or when he visited out-of-town friends, as I massaged his feet after a long day's work or while we watched DVDs, complimented him on how young he looked for his age—somehow, in his mind, I still fell short of being his ideal mate.

Of course, I know nobody's perfect. But I do believe that when a relationship ends, we're both at fault and yet—it's nobody's fault.

People are supposed to enter a relationship already happy and complete. We've all heard the saying, "Your partner is supposed to complement you, not complete you." While we are in a relationship to further enhance our happiness, it is not our responsibility to make the other person happy. My ex and I brought into our relationship some unresolved inner conflicts we had yet to face and resolve.

I admit, in hindsight, I was not assertive enough in the relationship. When friends were questioning why I didn't put up enough of a fuss whenever my ex went on trips without me, I merely shrugged my shoulders and said he needed time away from me (which he did) and I didn't want to be labeled as a complainer. The truth was, I was more than happy to watch his cats and we both needed a healthy dose of alone time. Still, I wished he and I took more trips together. My friends thought that made sense since my ex and I were both passionate about traveling. He claimed that we wouldn't travel well together. I thought, how could he make that assumption when, except for a few short trips we took, we had yet to take a long trip as a couple. So I chalked it up to his need to be a solo traveler and put the issue behind me.

I know I can't change the past, but looking back, I see his trips as a good thing as anyone in a relationship knows how beneficial alone time can be. In retrospect, I could have made myself less available, done more things on my own. I didn't have to live with the notion we had to be together 24/7. While I did have my own friends, my own hobbies and took my own trips, most of my free time was spent with my then boyfriend. In other words, I allowed what I swore would not happen again—that my life revolved around the person I was in a relationship with.

As I sit here now, I realize that the breakup had to happen in order for me to continue to work on myself. To pick up where I left off six years ago and continue to heal myself. This is what it means to have compassion for yourself.

To have compassion for the one who rejected you, hard as it may seem, is what's needed for you to move on. I think about my ex's warm and sensitive side (he does have one) and his need to release me and himself from the relationship. I didn't (and still don't) think he's a bad person. I think he did what he believed was the best he could for himself, the relationship and maybe, for me. Even to this day, I am grateful for all he's given me, the time we spent together and the laughs we shared, of which there were many. We hardly argued, mainly because I acquiesced to whatever he thought was right. But occasionally, I did stand firm when he raised his voice to me and he'd usually realize his unreasonable shortness with me and apologize.

I tried to acknowledge how accustomed he was to living his bachelor lifestyle since his divorce and understand his unwillingness to fully commit in the form of a live-in relationship and marriage. At some point, I temporarily abandoned the desire to be married myself, thinking a couple didn't need marriage to be together. Having never been married, I tried to put myself in my ex's shoes—what it must have felt like to be a product of divorce.

Meditation and yoga has helped me to empathize with my ex and understand how his past issues may have affected him. As I do challenging poses or when I'm distracted during meditation, the compassion I have for myself I try to extend toward my ex. The breakup, the time and distance between us, has ironically enabled me to learn to understand him more as I understand myself.

How does yoga and meditation help me become more compassionate? Whenever I attempt a challenging pose and I can't attain it (even though I succeeded before), I know it's because every day is different and I can't expect to excel in the same asana everyday. I'm not saying you shouldn't aim high or strive to attain a lofty goal on and off the mat. All I'm asking is for you to be realistic with your goals.

Whenever I sit in meditation and my mind wanders, I slowly bring my attention back to my breath. I feel compassion towards myself because I know I'm not perfect so that definitely takes the pressure off! Whether I'm practicing yoga or meditation, I'm not trying to compete with anyone—let alone compete with myself. I don't worry about beating my own sitting meditation record time, or whether I'm able to fully engage myself in crane pose—hoisting my whole body a few inches off the mat with only my hands and arms to support me—for a full minute. It's not about quantity of time; it's all about quality of experience.

It's also not about how many times I attend yoga class but how nourished and fulfilled I feel from my practice. It's not just the times you attend class that count. Time spent practicing yoga and meditation at home is invaluable. You are truly living the practice beyond the confines of a yoga studio or gym. The practice becomes you. You become the practice.

That's why you can't beat yourself up when you feel disappointed about not making it to yoga class or if you weren't able to fully execute a pose or were distracted during meditation. Just like you can't beat yourself up or fully blame your ex when a relationship ends.

Practicing self-compassion ensures you're clearing the path toward forgiveness—a state that you cannot force yourself into, but one that you will eventually find yourself in with time, patience and love.

Chapter 24:
Change Your Attitude,
Change Your Life

It's all in the attitude—or so we've heard. In the midst of heartache and in living, we learn that how we experience situations depends on our attitude. Just an hour after my breakup, my friend Jennifer told me, "When you change the way you look at things, the things you look at change." I've learned I can eliminate suffering just by changing my attitude.

When I think of attitude, some random thoughts about living and loving come to mind. For example, as I write this, my mind flashes back to the night of the breakup and how awful I felt. The scenes flash before me, some vivid, some rush by in a blur. But I realize I don't have to stay there. I am here now. I am safe.

It's natural to revisit the source of pain through memories, images and thoughts but know that that's all they are—just memories, images and thoughts. You can take yourself out of a place of unrest and into a place of peace through meditation and focusing on your breath.

When I find myself thinking sad or negative thoughts, I remind myself that I can put myself in and take myself out of my misery.

By embracing my pain as a growth experience, I'm fully utilizing the time, energy and emotion to changing my life for the better. I can choose to use suffering as a healing opportunity or ignore it altogether and pray that it goes away. But guess what? By doing so, I'm only inviting pain back in the form of another person and situation and I never really learned anything from my last experience. Asking God to take away the pain is like wishing you would never get better or wishing happiness would never come. And it will come eventually, with time.

I've learned that to get to that blissful place, I have to first do some tough inner work by overcoming emotional obstacles such as lack of self-worth and lack of self-love that are a deterrent to happiness.

I believe people who have utilized their pain as a tool for growth and healing have the most to gain as opposed to those who avoid suffering and seek only to find everlasting happiness from external sources that may not last. Asking God to take away your pain would be like refusing to allow the gift of peace to enter your life.

Chapter 25:
Smile Though Your Heart is Breaking: Laughing On & Off the Mat

Mere weeks after the breakup, Connie, a good friend of mine, urged that I adopt a new mantra—not just for getting over my ex but for life in general: "Fake it, till you make it."

So that swirled in my head until I came across the opportunity to practice those words in a most unusual but intriguing way.

Thanks to yoga classes offered by yoga instructor Linda Burkard and held at the Telfer Building in downtown Martinez, California, the concept of "Laughter Yoga" or "Hasya Yoga," introduced itself to me.

According to yoga instructor Bharat Shah of Sweet Therapeutic Yoga in Fremont:

> *Laughter Yoga is a deceptively simple yet very powerful and potentially even life-changing form of exercise that anybody can do, anytime, anywhere. Its core premise is that your body can and knows how to laugh, regardless of what your mind has to say. In*

short: Laughter Yoga is a body-mind approach to laughter, not something mind-body. The distinction is very important. Here you do not need to have a sense of humor, know jokes or even be happy. Laughter Yoga invites you to 'fake it' until it becomes real.

At a deeper level, it proves that pain can be overcome and also that we can all live at peace together no matter what. It teaches you to make happiness a choice and not a consequence.

Having read all that in a flyer, I made my way to class not knowing what to expect. This couldn't possibly be a class of strenuous poses. We were going to class to laugh whether we felt like it or not.

Shah infused his sense of humor into the class so that I felt like I was in a comedy club rather than yoga class. But, to me, the point of yoga, and of life for that matter, is to be open to all kinds of possibilities and expect the unexpected.

So we started the class with breathing exercises as we learned the importance of inhalations and exhalations and how laughter is beneficial when it comes from the belly. We laughed at anything and everything as we "role-played" our way through class assuming the movements of someone rushing through the airport while carrying our imaginary luggage to catch a flight, mowing the lawn, talking on an imaginary cell phone and so on. The point of these exercises was to be mindful of the fact that we can laugh through any situation.

As role-playing poses were intermittently sprinkled with laughter and standing forward bends, a feeling of lightheartedness was almost immediate.

Bharat continued to lead us into a series of breathing exercises that were also good for the stomach and throat. These exercises had us roaring like a lion then huffing and puffing which was great for relieving pent-up emotion. Frustrated with your ex? Roar like a lion!

We also did familiar poses such as Warrior, which Bharat said was a heart-opening, centering pose, and Tabletop, which we were encouraged to do with a smile or a laugh and I felt like a kid again, so carefree.

Laughter Yoga taught me to approach any situation without expectations. It also reminded me that all of yoga isn't physical. While there were a few postures, this practice of Hasya Yoga focused on breathing and how laughter enables you to relieve stress and depression. Bharat emphasized how you can incorporate Laughter Yoga into any activity like washing the dishes or doing the laundry, or driving. During these times when you may feel like bursting into tears, try laughing instead. Bharat said, "Fake it, till you make it," so that's what I did until I truly felt better by the end of the session.

Laughter makes me realize that all of life isn't sorrowful. If I laughed once, I can laugh again even in times of adversity. You can laugh at yourself in the face of stress and eventually the mind, body and spirit will laugh along with you.

Chapter 26:
What the Yogis Say

During my healing journey, I've had the honor of practicing with some of the most compassionate and genuine yoga instructors in the San Francisco Bay Area and I didn't have to travel far (although I do wish to go on a yoga retreat to India someday!) to become enlightened.

Bruce Guterman, who has been teaching yoga and Pilates for several years, draws students to his class with his practical, no-nonsense approach to yoga. His warm, inviting demeanor coupled with his melodic voice helps soothe the nerves as muscles stretch then relax from the stress of the day. Yoga philosophy, Bruce says, is really geared for those dealing with loss.

"It talks a lot about detachment and being able to stay centered within yourself amid all the outer turmoil of the world," he says.

Yoga chanting, he says, is one of the best ways to connect with the divine being within yourself. "This allows you to get in touch with your heart and the feelings you have in your heart. It's a great way to do personal healing. Through that, you can develop a relationship within yourself that helps with the healing process."

Meditation needn't be approached as a separate entity, Bruce says. "In yoga, you can do meditation with the intent of healing. Use music and yoga practice to process the painful feelings. The way to healing is to allow yourself to process or feel your pain."

Moving slowly and meditatively tunes you into the pain, he says. "People don't want to look inward. Just by going inward, you're taking a look at what's inside. By looking inward, you're realizing there's some pain there. You have to work through the pain. Allow yourself to be with the pain."

For most of us, it's hard to allow ourselves to feel pain, he notes. "Like a thorn coming out of the body. It hurts when it comes out, but after it's pulled out, the healing process naturally occurs." But Bruce acknowledges that it's a slow process and for some people, healing takes longer because they're avoiding the pain.

When we choose to open up to that heartbreak and pain, we choose to heal, he attests. There are different ways to do your healing work and some of those ways that complement yoga and meditation include attending support groups and seeking the comfort of others who are also undergoing a healing process. "When you want to build up your inner strength and self esteem, yoga is a great way to do that. It's not just for physical strength, but also inner balance and inner grounding," he adds.

Some yoga postures that aid in the manifestation of healing include Bow—either Full Bow or Side Bow— and Camel. As these poses open the rib cage, the heart also opens, he says.

Any kind of Pranayama or breathing exercise is good at opening the heart because you're working with breathing, working with the lungs, as well as the heart, Bruce adds.

"Eventually, the pain is going to work its way out," he assures. "It's a matter of time. It comes out bit by bit, in pieces, and in memories. Part of the process is working its way out over time." During this process, Bruce urges people to be good to themselves through self-love and self-compassion. Some ways of practicing this includes doing restorative poses such as forward bends, back bends and Child's pose.

"Over time, the feelings you have for that person will diminish as you do your healing work," he says. "It will be more like a memory."

It takes something like a breakup to force ourselves to grow. "The positive side of a breakup is you grow and mature. As long as you have a heart, it will be broken, but part of the natural growth process is growing and becoming more solid within yourself and developing a stronger sense of who you are as an individual person."

Wendy Beckerman of East Bay Yoga, who teaches Anusara-inspired yoga and mindfulness meditation, has this to say:

> There are five generally accepted forms of yoga, one being raja yoga, or meditation. The others are bhakti yoga of devotion, karma yoga of selfless service, jnana yoga of wisdom through study, and hatha yoga or physical asana practice. What each of these forms of yoga has in common is cultivation of greater awareness. In mindfulness meditation, we choose a present-moment point of focus such as breathing or

body sensations. When we notice the mind has wandered, we acknowledge whatever has arisen, such as a thought or emotion, and intentionally return our awareness to the point of focus with an attitude of kindness to ourselves.

This method is particularly helpful for those dealing with heartbreak as negative thoughts and emotions tend to surface causing the afflicted person to become distracted from the task at hand.

I know first-hand what it's like to not be able to focus on my work deadlines or enjoy a get together with friends simply because I allow thoughts about my ex to invade my emotional space. This always results in serious, adverse effects on my ability to appreciate whatever gifts I am offered at the present moment.

So Wendy encouraged me to ask myself, "If I wasn't obsessing about this, what would I be doing? What matters most in this moment? You're not pushing your problems away. You're redirecting your focus so you're not getting swallowed up by your emotions."

So what do you do with your emotions when they are powerful but not necessarily obsessive? Wendy suggests we continue to cultivate mindfulness by being with our emotions. "If we push an emotion away, it becomes more powerful," she says. "We're accepting it because it's happening and allowing it to ripple through our experience."

By connecting and being aware with the hurtful feelings, not denying or resisting them and just letting our feelings be, we're actually empowering ourselves by giving ourselves a chance to face our emotions bravely.

Yoga and meditation are powerful tools for helping us heal from obsessive thoughts that overwhelm us and disable us from functioning in our lives. In Wendy's Anusara-style yoga classes, as students' minds are occupied with trying to stay focused on precise alignment of body, they are also practicing being in alignment with themselves.

"We're either moving towards feeling connected with who we really are or celebrating that connection that's already present," Wendy says. As you are attempting yoga poses, you are accepting yourself and your efforts in a nonjudgmental way. This is what I can achieve at this moment. Who I am is a deeper matter.

Yoga's meditative powers help to reframe thoughts stemming from the concept of "someone rejecting you." If, in fact, someone broke up with you, after the deed is done, it is in the past where it should stay. How you treat yourself going forward is what matters now. Yoga and meditation empowers you to stay firmly rooted in the present—a state of acceptance of who you are.

"Who you really are is whole, beautiful 'unrejectable,'" Wendy says affirmatively. "Nobody is rejected. When you feel rejected—you're simply not connected with who you really are which is part of the game of being human."

A disconnection ensues—an inability to connect with your inner light. Here's where heart-opening postures can help us reconnect with that light inside. Since we hold a lot of emotions in our bodies, we can turn to physically opening poses to allow ourselves to reveal that light.

"You can be uncovering what is it you've been covering," Wendy says. Some of these postures include a forward bend or Child's pose. "It's appropriate to go inward and be with sadness and loss."

Just as there aren't miracle pills to help you heal a broken heart, heart-opening poses are not a quick fix and are to be done gradually as you heal. The whole point of healing is to work towards recovery not striving for immediate relief. Just as it takes time to heal emotionally, your body needs to move at its own pace. It's your body, Wendy advises, only you can choose how much you can do at any given time.

"Yoga practice is about being kind to yourself, receiving your practice as a gift, an act of love, as nourishment," she says. "Heart-opening exercises can be very powerful and should be done when you're ready by tuning into your own sensitivity about what you're ready for."

It's important to recognize that there are different layers of healing for different people and that the amount of time it takes to heal varies depending on the person, she says. Those dealing with the loss of a loved one can be led by the light of awareness to thought and emotion. "Take a step back and see it for what it is and create an opportunity to carve a new pathway," Wendy says.

She taught me that instead of saying "I was rejected," which amplifies the incorrect and negative concept of you as a rejected person, stay connected with your emotions and try saying "I *feel* rejected."

Feelings are fleeting and therefore impermanent. They don't define who you are so they're not permanent. Mindfulness teaches us to allow ourselves to acknowledge feeling rejected as opposed to being rejected as a person. "When we work with being present with emotions during meditation, it can be useful to notice where the emotion is felt in the body," Wendy says.

Feelings, thoughts and emotions rise up to the surface and we, in turn, rise up to face them, allowing them to run their course. But these all-too-human feelings, thoughts and emotions of rejection are not who we are. We decide who we are and who we want to be.

ॐ

Chapter 27:
A Yogi's Healing Journey
After Heartbreak

As I heal from heartbreak, I've had the great fortune to practice with spiritually insightful yoga instructors including the ones I mentioned earlier. Sarah Pascual is one of them. After attending a yoga session with Sarah, I emerge with hope, my spirits renewed. In her classes, Sarah emphasizes the use of *prana* or breath to connect with your body, your heart, your mind, your soul. She encourages people to be one with the earth by placing hands and feet on the bamboo floor of the yoga studio while in Downward Dog pose or on the grass during an outdoor "Yoga in the Park" session at Civic Park in downtown Walnut Creek.

The breath, Sarah says, creates space—enabling you to receive more—blessings, gifts that life can offer. Taking deep breaths not only allows us to ease into each pose but allows us to be open to receive more breath and with it, more positive energy.

Sarah and I bonded over our shared sorrow—we both had been the recipients of pain from breakups at about the same time. When I told her I was writing this book not only to heal myself and to understand the process, but also to reach out to others, she willingly shared her own story of heartbreak. After hearing her story, I realized that when a lover tells us "It's over," we shouldn't automatically berate ourselves. It happens to even to best of us.

Over lunch one day, Sarah admitted to me that she "went through the worst breakup last year," an experience I could wholeheartedly relate to. I sat up straight, literally at the edge of my seat, my lunch growing cold by the minute. I wanted to know how anyone could break up with this good-natured girl—beautiful inside and out—and how she managed to survive her grief. She had my full attention.

They were together for two years, Sarah and her guy. "We just had a beautiful connection. We connected on all levels. I felt he was The One at the time," she says, wistfully. When you're in love, you see qualities you want to see in the object of your affection and the good qualities become amplified, she says. In your eyes, your beloved can do no wrong.

The breakup, she says, was his decision. "I still don't have a clear answer why." Her intuition was telling her that he wanted to see other people.

Just as I felt some tension, some unexplained change in the dynamic of my relationship with my ex before our breakup; Sarah says she felt it, too.

"Energetically, I felt a shift—we had a little fallout, something you shouldn't have an argument about. I could tell something else was boiling. He called me over. He was sitting in his room. We held each other for a real long time."

She had no idea what he wanted to talk about but then she saw something in his tearful eyes, which still confused her. "He said, 'We basically needed to end things. We're just not on the same page.' I was bawling now, in a state of shock. We continued to stay there, crying." While she believed that her guy was no doubt in love with her, she surmised that he was scared of commitment. "I'm finding a lot of men are."

"When we broke up, I was a mess. I cried for days. I didn't want to be alone. I still taught yoga and still had to wake up and get myself together and carry on." She couldn't believe that she had someone with whom she had dedicated her life and heart to and now, he was gone.

A lot of time was spent on the phone with girlfriends trying to figure out what went wrong, what she could've done and second-guessing herself.

In a relationship, when one should be taking some time to do things to make yourself happy, you end up sacrificing things to be with that loved one, leaving virtually little or no time for yourself, she says.

Just like me, Sarah couldn't just let things go. After the breakup, she continued to hang out with her ex as friends—practicing yoga together, going dancing, having dinner at his house. "When I left (his house), it was a like a breakup again. I continued to torture myself." Then she realized, things had to change and it had to start with her. "You have to take care of yourself—no one else can take care of you," she says.

This meant keeping her distance—from an occasional e-mail to no contact with her ex for six months. She started dating again and diving into her passions such as yoga and surfing. Then one day as she was blow-drying her hair, she had a sudden realization. Sarah remembers:

This huge clarity, this huge gratitude. I was thankful for him breaking up with me because if he didn't break up with me, I wouldn't know what heartbreak felt like to that extent. I wouldn't be meeting people and learning about myself—truly being okay with just myself without having a man to make me happy. I wake up in the morning and it's just me."

When you are independent and completely okay with being alone, it's (sometimes) scary and couldn't be any more uncomfortable. But I think you need to grow as an individual. When you have that and meet a person who's on the same level, when you're not too needy and not expecting that person to entertain you all the time, you have freedom. You come together to share that togetherness.

I think nobody wants to truly hurt somebody. It's a growing and learning experience for them as well. He had to do what he had to do for himself to be happy, even if that meant breaking my heart. I honor him for doing that.

Sarah affirms that when we come to the realization that something isn't serving us in life, we need to explore why, and then let it go. You can't control how the other person thinks and acts, you can only control and take care of yourself. When one person doesn't fully commit to the relationship, even though the other person is committed, that person who doesn't want to commit is doing a disservice by remaining in the relationship. By leaving, that person has made the decision to take care of himself just as the person who was on the receiving end of hurt needs to take care of herself.

What really helped her through the breakup was yoga—her saving grace. Still, she admitted, it was hard to get herself onto the yoga mat. When she did, she would just cry. Even harder still was the fact that despite her heartache, she still had to teach yoga class—still had to be a pillar of strength, a beacon of light for her students. "Once I just sat and closed my eyes and focused on the breath and the layers started to peel off. My heart started to calm down."

She began to return to her own body, back to her true self after yoga practice which prevented her from being distracted by external things and messages that kept her from tuning within. Performing movements such as Warrior pose while connecting to her breath helped her tap into her inner strength. When in doubt, she says, always come back to the breath. "That's where healing comes from," Sarah affirms.

In her classes, she encourages students to move freely in tandem with the breath—so that breath and movement are one. She likes to connect movement and breath with elements of nature: ocean, water, fire, earth, breath, air. The breath is a powerful healing tool.

"It's a beautiful thing when we bring our awareness to the breath," she says. "Everything starts to soften, emotions start to settle."

Distractions, hurts, memories from the past may still be there but by connecting ourselves to our breath, we're not allowing the past to distract us or derail us from journeying toward our true self.

You can find another relaxing and enjoyable activity, besides yoga, that helps you appreciate life. For others, that could be walking, running or riding a bike. For Sarah, surfing has been a form of meditation.

When she's out there on the water, she says, there's this huge force that's very powerful, yet very graceful. In surfing, just as in life, you take risks, including the risk of hitting your head on the surfboard and the risk of opening your heart to love again. "It's all about trust. All you can do is breathe and be in the present moment and let it all unravel." If you don't stay connected to your breath, your mind and body go elsewhere—to inner and outer destructive places the mind, body and spirit shouldn't go like back to past hurts.

By surrendering yourself to your breath—wonderful inhalations and equally powerful, toxin-releasing exhalations, you're giving your body so much bliss and awareness. "We release old habits and emotions and past traumas. I feel a lot better inside myself, finding true compassion for my ex because he's human as well. He has wants and needs. I hope he truly finds that contentment within himself."

A huge part of moving on, Sarah says, is learning how to be selfish for yourself. "I really appreciate me time. When I was with him, I didn't appreciate it before. I like going home and being in a space that's so healing and so grounding. Without the heartache, we wouldn't know the love. I received pain as a gift. At the time of the breakup, you didn't know why this was happening, but in time, you'll know."

Chapter 28:
From Heartbreaking to Heart-Opening

As I approached another birthday, I didn't quite dread the occasion as I had a year ago when my heartbreak was still so raw. Instead, I approached this birthday with as much spontaneity as I could muster.

To kick off my birthday weekend, Stephanie, one of my closest friends, and I took a day trip to Half Moon Bay as we were also celebrating her birthday. It was quite bittersweet. The previous birthdays I celebrated with my ex, whose birthday was the day before mine, and to mark the occasion we chose locations that were near an ocean or a lake. One year it was camping on Sonoma State Beach, another year we spent our birthdays watching the Pacific Ocean sunset in Monterey as a bagpiper played Celtic music near the seashore at the Inns at Spanish Bay.

Another birthday was celebrated with a refreshing dip on a small cove along Lake Tahoe. On my last birthday celebration with him, we strolled along the Embarcadero enjoying a spectacular view of the San Francisco Bay and later continued our celebration with a paella dinner at a restaurant on Belden Lane in San

Francisco, followed by late night cocktails and jazz music at our favorite hangout, Café Claude.

So, of course, as Stephanie and I sat and enjoyed a delicious, piping hot cup of clam chowder, complemented with a breathtaking view of the Pacific Ocean, I couldn't help but remember my ex.

But the sooner my yogic self, my "Buddha nature" kicked in, the more I became aware that it was the present. I immediately took note of the scene around me—people walking their dogs along the sandy cove, seagulls soaring through the clouds framing the setting sun, the sight of an adorable Yellow Labrador delighting us with his sweet face, the warmth of the sun on my cheek.

"I'm thoroughly enjoying this moment," I told Stephanie, almost whispering the revelation to myself. "It's so beautiful."

We had visited Half Moon Bay nursery earlier, which Stephanie described as her plant heaven. She was right. In fact, as soon as she drove onto the highway leading to Half Moon Bay, I suddenly felt the shift—the relaxing feeling I usually get when transitioning from cityscape to seascape. As we were enveloped with mist, my spine tingled with anticipation of journeying near the ocean.

Once we arrived at the nursery, we entrenched ourselves into a sea of green and colorful foliage— snapdragons, hydrangeas, roses, hibiscus, orchids, bonsai, citrus and bamboo plants. The place overwhelmed me yet I surrendered, allowed myself to be consumed by the breath of plant life connecting me to nature, reminding me to slow down, to appreciate life one breath at a time.

So that was what I did—allowed my inhalations and exhalations I so carefully execute in yoga class to work its magic beyond the yoga mat. With each breath I took, I released the past and made room for the present and whatever blessings the future would hold.

Later, for an early dinner at Sam's Chowder House, Stephanie suddenly fixated on a figure not in my accessible vantage point.

"There's a cute guy sitting behind you," she whispered. Of course, not wanting to embarrass myself, I simply smiled as Stephanie took out her new Smart Phone and announced with a knowing look, "I'm going to take a picture of you."

As we giggled like schoolgirls, Stephanie kept taking a series of shots as I directed her. "Make sure I'm not the center of the photo."

She knew what I meant and intended to include the guy whom she later dubbed the "Mystery Man" in photo captions. This was also a way I could "steal" a look at him since I couldn't actually turn around and stare now, could I? With all the giddy commotion we were already making, it would be obvious.

Although I caught a glimpse of him as we headed out, alas, a romance was not to be. Or would there?

"Darn it! I should've introduced the two of you," Stephanie lamented as we reviewed the photos back in her car. "I should've said, 'Excuse me, but I'd like to introduce you to a friend of mine.' Let's go back."

"No! You wouldn't dare," I pleaded, knowing all too well she would do it.

"But he was alone," she insisted.

"Yeah, but it didn't mean he was single," I countered. "Did you see him on his cell phone?"

"Yeah, he seemed to texting someone," Stephanie said, going over the photos she took. "Check out his furrowed brow. Maybe someone stood him up. So intense. Come on. Let's go back."

I sighed. "What are you now, my pimp?"

She mock-glanced at me. "I'd rather be called your matchmaker."

Finally, we "settled" on situating ourselves at a scenic spot nearby taking turns photographing each other with the ocean in the background while the "Mystery Man" looked on from his table. Once, I caught him with a knowing smirk on his face. My heart pounded. *He knows*, I thought.

At the end of the day, we left the lulling sounds of the crashing waves of Half Moon Bay behind us as we ventured back to the East Bay, back to reality.

I learned a valuable lesson from our adventure—that I didn't need my ex or memories of him, or the company of a man to be happy on my birthday or any day for that matter. I was alive, inhaling fresh ocean air into my lungs and I had the love of a wonderful family and friends as evidenced by the greetings I received my entire birthday week.

Another lesson learned: I didn't need to be in a relationship to experience romance. While I didn't exchange glances or words with the "Mystery Man," the giggles, giddiness, heart-tingling palpitations I felt as Stephanie and I concocted possible scenarios about the guy, I had experienced feeling good about romance again. In other words, as my birthday weekend loomed ahead, as I slowly released my emotional grip on my ex, I prepared and eagerly anticipated falling in love again. I realized romance can come in many forms from stolen glances with a stranger to an encounter with someone you find attractive and whom you may never see again.

We create romance in our lives. There is hope after heartbreak. Heartbreak and being in love, pain and joy, remind us we are living, breathing creatures. I had to have my heart broken to truly prepare myself to love again. It's just as yoga instructor Sarah Pascual says in her classes: "Ask yourself—what can you let go in order to receive?"

Inhale the present, exhale the past and receive. My birthday this year became a breathday.

It's going to be a great year.

Chapter 29:
Looking Back
to Look Forward

There's been this great debate among my friends for years regarding infidelity. Some say if they found out their significant other cheated on them, which type of cheating would they most likely endure? Physical or emotional cheating? Which one was forgivable? Unforgivable?

"I'd rather my husband say that it was just sex, Babe, you're the one I love," said a friend of mine.

"Yeah," agreed another friend. "I'd take that over emotional cheating any day."

"Why?" I couldn't help but wonder.

"Because emotional cheating is harder to take," she explained. "Once he gives his heart away to someone else, that's it."

It's hard to say whether my ex emotionally-cheated on me. One of the reasons he broke up with me was because he said that I didn't believe him when he claimed he didn't have feelings for the woman the first time I asked him about it.

Just right before the breakup, when the woman's presence was predominant, a friend of mine had said,

"Maybe they both shared the same feelings but hadn't quite admitted it to each other yet." Who knows if they had feelings for each other long before I came into the picture but the timing wasn't quite right for them to be together?

Seems like my own intuition broke the news to me first. But whether or not my ex emotionally cheated on me, the fact was, he was interested in the woman. Even though I didn't ask him to choose between her and me, he made his choice.

"You think I'm going to give up her friendship," he said, angrily, the night of the breakup. "I've known her longer than I've known you. She's a wonderful, wonderful girl." He made his choice. He chose her.

A year after the breakup, it still hurts to think about it but it only hurts if: a) if I allow myself to think about it and b) if I dwell on the thought and allow the thought to hurt me. So, I try not to think about it. But I'm only human. Yoga teaches me not to be hard on myself, to allow myself to feel whatever I'm feeling and then let it go. If I think about that dreadful night it's not to torture myself, but to remind myself that I survived. That I'm healing. That I'm at a better place now.

Accepting that the man I loved with all my heart gave his heart to someone else has been a fact I've had to live with every day. The reality that I love someone who made the choice not to be with me has transformed my thinking from not being loved to having the freedom to love again. Just as one of his friends told me soon after the breakup: "He has set you free." Now, it's a choice I'm making to love myself first.

A few months ago, one of my closest, dearest friends revealed something to me that put my whole heartbreak experience into perspective. She has generously given me permission to share her story as long as I don't disclose her identity. My married friend said she thought sharing her story would help others heal with compassion. She believes the broken-hearted should know that it's not easy either for those who may have cheated emotionally.

My longtime friend tearfully admitted to me that she had feelings for another man and that they went on a few dates. While she claims her relationship with this man had never crossed the physical realm, this interlude somehow brought back romance into her life.

By the time she confessed her "emotional infidelity" to me, she said it was over for her even though the man still wanted to pursue the relationship.

"I had to stop it," she cried. I was quiet on the other end of the telephone conversation. I didn't know what to say at first. How I wish I could've seen the expression on her face. It's necessary to have these kinds of conversations face-to-face, I thought. But, she couldn't bear to keep it all bottled up inside her for much longer. The guilt was tearing her up inside.

All the while my mind kept racing. On the one hand, I could've told her, "How could you, after you've seen what I've been through?" How could I show compassion for a close friend who emotionally cheated on her loving, sensitive husband and devoted father to her children? But my friend was in turmoil. She didn't know what she could do to redeem herself. The guilt consumed her.

That was when my brain snapped at the "G" word. Guilt. I couldn't stand it whenever I heard someone rattle remorsefully over what they did. I used to be one of those people. I knew that the guilt would hover over their entire lives effectively killing their chance at happiness and forgiveness.

Instead, I listened to my friend as I gathered as much compassion as I could muster. What would I do if I were in her shoes? Then, I thought, I wouldn't do such a thing in the first place. But, the reality hit me. It could happen to anyone. Anyone could be capable of emotional cheating.

Immediately, I thought of the times when, while I was still with my ex, that I daydreamed about being with other guys, especially during the times when my ex wasn't particularly treating me so kindly.

"You're only human," I said, calming her down, trying my best to assuage her guilt. "You lost your dad last year and your kids are away at school. You're looking for someone to love."

"But I love my husband," my friend said of the man she has been with since she was 18. She admitted the romance had gone out of her marriage, but it wasn't her intention to stray or hurt her husband.

"I know you love him," I told her.

"He'll never know about the other guy," my friend said, choking back more tears. "If he found out, it would kill him."

Of course, right as my friend was revealing this "transgression" to me, I was still reeling from the shock of my ex falling for someone else. I didn't want to mention this to her. After all, she was feeling awful for what she did—what she could have done. As a friend, I wanted to comfort her, make her feel good about herself again.

"You have the intense capacity to love," I said. "Is that such a bad thing? You loved your Dad so much but when he died, you had so much love to give. This guy was the lucky recipient of that love."

"But why couldn't I shower my husband with all that love?" she asked.

"Because you love him already and I know you still do. But you were looking for other people to lavish your affection on and he happened to be there. There's nothing wrong with spreading love if you have so much of it that you're practically bursting at the seams to give away as much of it as you can." Mind you, giving love to others doesn't mean physically giving yourself to them.

My theory into my friend's actions surprised me a bit. Did that mean my ex have so much love to give that he had to give more away to someone else and if loving isn't a crime, had he been absolved from any wrongdoing?

"Look, nothing else happened, right?" I continued. "Be grateful for that. Be thankful for what this experience has taught you about love and about life. That nothing stays the same. So, maybe you can't recapture that ecstatic state you first had with your husband years ago. You still have your marriage. Maybe this is a sign you and your husband need to start dating again after the hard work of raising two kids for 20 years. I think it's about time you need to take some time for just the two of you."

To my relief, I believe my friend started to calm down. She realized she wasn't a bad person for being attracted to someone else besides her husband.

So my thoughts returned to my ex. I don't blame him for ending our relationship. I could easily blame the woman for getting between me and my ex, but I won't anymore. I think that's proof of how much I've grown from my heartbreak.

Learning about my friend's experience has been a lesson in humility. It's humbling to know that while my ex gave his heart away to someone else, the fact is, it could've been the other way around. I could've left my ex for someone else.

Who knows why we may experience a gravitational pull toward another human being even while the one we're with has been nothing short of loving and supportive? It may just simply mean we are capable of loving so much that we long to spread it around. We're human after all. Still, it's *how* we spread it around that determines our fate. So, I've tried with all my might to approach my own situation with as much understanding as I had shown to my friend.

"Please forgive yourself," I urged her. I now forgive myself for being angry at my ex. I forgive him for his callous way of breaking up with me. I even forgive the woman who came between us. After all, what good does it do for me to continue to be angry?

In order to move forward, I need to reflect back, not to lay any blame, not to look back with regret over loving my ex or lament over a list of should haves or should not haves, but to reflect on the lessons I've learned and am still learning.

We are all vulnerable to pain and to love and both pain and love may lead us to do crazy things if we're not mindful of our thoughts and actions. There is a little bit of a yogi in my friend who's never set foot on a yoga mat. She was mindful enough to realize she loved her husband with all her heart and wanted to stay with him.

I was mindful enough to know that while it's perfectly acceptable to cry oceans of tears over my breakup, it's not acceptable to wish my ex or the woman any harm or deem them unforgivable. I only bask in the glory of knowing I'll be okay, that I've survived and that I continue to heal. That same capacity to love that I told my friend she had would ultimately find its way back into my own heart once again.

In fact, I believe that love has been there all along—waiting until it's ready again.

Chapter 30:
Dipping Your Toes
in the Pool of Life

The lessons don't end when the heartache is over.

By this time on the journey toward recovery from heartbreak, it's probably safe to assume I've learned some valuable lessons along the way. I've learned that personal growth can be attained through experiencing emotional pain. Despite my distress, yoga and meditation have saved me. I believe that there are some life lessons that you can only learn from experiencing heartbreak—more than any other type of painful situation. If I didn't love my ex, then I wouldn't experience pain. If I didn't experience pain, then I wouldn't have turned to yoga and meditation and have the need for self-discovery and self-love. In other words, I would have missed out on the wisdom that my pain— the knowing, inner teacher—was trying to teach me.

For instance, this past year I've tried many more different yoga styles than I ever thought I possibly could. This process of experimenting and exploring allowed me to discover different avenues to well being and aspects of myself. There are different types of yoga to suit various moods and personalities. I now know that, on any given day, I can choose to practice a style of yoga that's suitable to my physical and emotional needs. Whenever I need a pick-me-up energizing practice or need to remind myself to go with the flow, I choose to do a more vigorous Vinyasa yoga practice. On my "off" days, I'd rather attend a gentle yoga or the blissful restorative yoga class rather than skip yoga altogether.

While this past year I've embraced yoga and meditation in a way I'd never have before, at the start of Fall 2010, I embarked on a yogic crusade, a "Yoga Boot Camp" of sorts, but not in the extreme, Army-training approach.

I finally attended classes at Tierra Yoga, an eco-friendly yoga studio in Hercules after attending the studio's grand opening in January. I signed up for the 10-class special and my personal challenge was to complete 10 classes before the special expired at the end of September. More than half of the month had gone by but I decided to go for it.

And so, I did. Even if that meant taking a couple of classes a day, I found that it wasn't as exhaustive or physically draining as I thought it would be. I kept telling myself "Isn't this the most un-yogic thing I could do—push myself through an intense yoga practice just to take advantage of a good deal?"

What I no doubt experienced was intense but immensely gratifying. I tried a smorgasbord of offerings—Ashtanga, Vinyasa, Gentle Yoga, Yin Yoga, and something called Ashtanga—Rocket I which I discovered was one of the most physically-challenging of all the yoga classes I've attended in all my years of practice. Yet, I didn't feel like I was forcing myself in any way. What I discovered—as I attempted and succeeded at the headstand—and the dozens of

Chaturanga Dandasana (Push-Up pose) to Upward Facing Dog poses, and vigorous movements in Sun Salutations, was that I was fearless. I could—if I freed my body and mind to the task at hand—set myself on the course toward success.

I learned that success means different things to different people. You define what success means to you. So what if you can't attempt a headstand in class? I couldn't do a headstand in class one day, but later, in the privacy of my home, I succeeded, not just once, but twice. I knew I could do it, but in my own time without pressure by the yoga instructor or pressure to compete with other students. That's what yoga has taught me—to respect and honor my mind and body's ability to do things at its own time and place, at its own rhythm and pace.

Even my nephew, Christian, accompanied me to yoga class. After I tried to persuade him for months to try it, he attended a couple of classes with me at Tierra Yoga. While his very first yoga class was Ashtanga—a bit on the challenging side to say the least—he flowed just fine and even surrendered to Child's pose when it got too intense. I was so proud of him. I was grateful for Ilia, Tierra Yoga's owner and yoga instructor, and her gentle, nurturing guidance and instruction to Christian even though I knew Ilia's specialty was this rigorous, dynamic practice, surely a departure from the gentle prodding she offered my nephew. But, then again, that was Ilia—a strong, energetic yogi with a touch of tenderness.

Christian joined me for Ilia's version of Gentle Yoga (she had to sub this class) a week later and he found that this was more his preference.

"Christian is such a cool teenager," Ilia cooed. "You're such a cool auntie for bringing him to yoga."

Just as I got a chance to try new yoga styles in a short span of time, I continued on this path during my Fall Fearless Female mode. The Vinyasa Flow classes where I flowed from one pose to the next with vigor and intensity—literally going with the flow with virtually no pauses between poses—seemed to influence me off the mat as well.

Over the summer, around the time of the Half Moon Bay Mystery Man encounter, I met a guy who intrigued me and captivated my attention in a way I hadn't been captivated in a long time. While we had a few interactions during a summer writing class in 2010, the quality of our encounters was thought provoking. We talked about writing, our backgrounds, our mutual interest in his Irish-American culture, our sports teams (he's a Boston Red Sox fan!)—and the conversation flowed naturally, organically. I felt I could be myself with this guy. He seemed nice and unassuming.

We talked about getting together to talk about writing and have been exchanging e-mails. While I don't know what will become of this friendship, an interaction such as this has given me hope that I could open my heart again. I know I need to slow down and savor the experience. Be thoroughly in the moment and enjoy the ride.

Friends have told me to relax, have fun, hangout and see where this ride will take me. A wonderful friendship could result out of this, or, who knows, maybe more? I need to not worry about the hurts of the past and what words or actions may trigger those past hurts. I can't even worry about the future either—being anxious about the past and the future takes away the beauty of this present experience.

My attraction to this man is indeed a huge, glorious step toward healing and moving forward. This is the first serious "crush" I've had in a long time and it makes me both excited and nervous. I don't know what the future holds, but as I slowly learn to open my heart again and trust the process of life, the future appears promising.

And, by the way, the present isn't too shabby either.

ॐ

Chapter 31:
With Each Breath

After intensely hot mid-October days, the Bay Area finally welcomed the inevitable cool break that ushered in the fall season.

I celebrated the long-awaited (although others preferred the extended summer) season change by taking a walk on the Albany Waterfront Trail. An overcast drizzle complete with bay breeze bathed my uncovered head and face but I didn't mind as I walked along the trail adorned with graffiti-laden rocks and concrete plastered with mosaic tiles in the shape of a heart. These makeshift memorials seemed to be lasting tributes to the various people who gathered there to leave some kind of milestone, some kind of legacy behind—to leave their mark on the world.

I found that one way I could make my own mark on the world is through every breath I take. As I breathed in the morning bay air, I felt I was taking a collective breath with the rest of the living, breathing world. I experienced a sense of oneness as we inhaled and exhaled together.

We all want to be happy. Whether it's the seagulls gliding across the sky or feral cats looking for their morning meal, the dogs eagerly immersing themselves into the cool waters of the bay with their owners looking on—we long to be happy in this life.

My heart, mind and body felt extremely free that morning and with every step I took, I connected to the earth.

I thought—almost with horrific fearlessness that grabbed hold of me and wouldn't let go—that if tripped over a rock on this dirt path and hit my head—I'd still be happy. Before me were the Campanile tower in Berkeley, downtown Oakland, the Bay Bridge, Treasure Island, the downtown San Francisco cityscape, the Golden Gate Bridge and a bit of Marin County all within my range of sight. And, oh, what a glorious sight!

So, I walked in happiness knowing I have the love of a wonderful family and devoted friends. I write satisfying stories—fiction and nonfiction. I live a full life as a writer and journalist as I teach others to write their own life stories. I have a promising career as a fitness professional with the hope that I may teach yoga and reach others someday, as others have reached me. I have met and continue to meet some interesting people, traveled and hope to still travel to magnificent places.

I have loved with all my heart. I've been blessed to give and receive love. I long, with every fiber of my being, to write and publish more books, to touch and change lives through my writing. I continue to pray and trust that life will provide me with my highest good and that divine right order will prevail.

I am on the path to loving myself more and more each day. I am now ready and open and willing to receive love again because there is so much more love I can give to that special someone. And when the time is right it will be worth the wait.

References

Colgrove, Melba, Ph.D., Bloomfield, Harold H., M.D., McWilliams, Peter. *How to Survive the Loss of a Love.* Prelude Press.

Hay, Louise L. *Power Thought Cards.* Hay House, Inc., 1999.

Kasl, Charlotte, Ph. D. *If the Buddha Dated: A Handbook for Finding Love on a Spiritual Path.* Penguin/Arkana, 1999.

Turlington, Christy. *Living Yoga: Creating a Life Practice.* Hyperion Books, 2002.

Vanzant, Iyanla. *Faith in the Valley: Lessons for Women on the Journey to Peace.* Fireside Books, 1996

Wilcox, Adele. *Mending Broken Hearts: Meditations for Finding Peace and Hope After Heartbreak.* Penguin Putnam, 1999.

Wilson, Kimberly. *Hip Tranquil Chick: A Guide to Life On and Off the Yoga Mat.* Inner Ocean Publishing, 2006.

Wood, Bliss. *Empowering Your Life with Yoga.* Alpha Books, 2004

Resources

East Bay Yoga
Wendy Beckerman
www.eastbayyoga.com
510-710-710

The Center for Holistic Well Being
Individual Counseling, Support and Growth Groups,
Yoga and Meditation classes and workshops
5433 Valley View Road, El Sobrante, CA 94803
510-222-8150

Full Body Yoga Studio
Bruce Guterman, M.A., RYT, CMT
Fullbodyyoga@gmail.com
www.Fullbodyyoga.com

Sarah Pascual
Certified Yoga Instructor and Massage Therapist
925-395-6858
blissfullyoga@gmail.com

Tierra Yoga
2192 Railroad Ave.
Hercules, CA 94547
www.tierrayoga.com

YMendoza Photography
Yolanda Mendoza, photographer
510-435-4357
www.YMendozaPhotography.com

Linda Burkard
Certified Yoga Therapist
http://lindaburkardyoga.blogspot.com

Suggested Reading

Beland, Nicole. *Girl Seeks Bliss: Zen and the Art of Modern Life Maintenance.* Plume Book, 2005.

Ban Breathnach, Sarah. *The Simple Abundance Companion: Following Your Authentic Path to Something More.* Warner Books, Inc. 2000.

Chodron, Pema. *When Things Fall Apart: Heart Advice for Difficult Times.* Shambhala Publications, Inc. 2000.

Colgrove, Melba, Ph.D., Bloomfield, Harold H., M.D., McWilliams, Peter. *How to Survive the Loss of a Love.* Prelude Press.

Das, Lama Surya. *Letting Go of the Person You Used to Be: Lessons on Change, Loss, and Spiritual Transformation.* Broadway Books, 2003.

Hansen Grey, Carol. *Simple Healing Tools: On the Path to Personal Empowerment and Inner Peace.* Open Heart Press, 2009.

Hay, Louise L. *Heart Thoughts: A Treasury of Inner Wisdom.* 1990.

Hay, Louise L. *Power Thought Cards.* Hay House, Inc., 1999.

Hemingway, Mariel. *Healthy Living from the Inside Out.* HarperCollins, 2007
His Holiness, the Dalai Lama, Cutler, Howard C., M.D. The Art of Happiness. Riverhead Books, 1998.

Kasl, Charlotte, Ph. D. *If the Buddha Dated: A Handbook for Finding Love on a Spiritual Path.* Penguin/Arkana, 1999.

Kingma, Daphne Rose. *Loving Yourself: Four Steps to a Happier You.* Conari Press, 2004.

Lasater, Judith, Ph.D., P.T. *Living Your Yoga: Finding the Spiritual in Everyday Life.* Rodmell Press, 2000.

Moran, Victoria. *My Yoga Journal: Guided Reflections through Writing.* Walking Stick Press, 2002.

Nelsen, Jane. *Serenity: Simple Steps for Recovering Peace of Mind, Real Happiness, and Great Relationships.* Conari Press, 2008.

Norwood, Robin. *Daily Meditations for Women Who Love Too Much.* Jeremy P. Tarcher/Putnam. 1997

NurrieStearns, Mary and Rick. *Yoga for Anxiety: Meditations and Practices for Calming the Body and Mind.* New Harbinger Publications, Inc. 2010.

Orloff, Judith, M.D. *Emotional Freedom: Liberate Yourself from Negative Emotions and Transform Your Life.* Harmony Books, 2009.

Ross, Steve. *Happy Yoga: 7 Reasons Why There's Nothing to Worry About.* HarperCollins, 2003.

Turlington, Christy. *Living Yoga: Creating a Life Practice.* Hyperion Books, 2002.

Vanzant, Iyanla. *Faith in the Valley: Lessons for Women on the Journey to Peace.* Fireside Books, 1996.

Vanzant, Iyanla. *Until Today! Daily Devotions for Spiritual Growth and Peace of Mind.* Fireside Books, 2000.

Weintraub, Amy. *Yoga for Depression: A Compassionate Guide to Relieve Suffering Through Yoga.* Broadway Books, 2004.

Wilcox, Adele. *Mending Broken Hearts: Meditations for Finding Peace and Hope After Heartbreak.* Penguin Putnam, 1999.

Williamson, Marianne. *A Return to Love: Reflections on the Principles of A Course in Miracles.* HarperPerennial, 1996.

Wilson, Kimberly. *Hip Tranquil Chick: A Guide to Life On and Off the Yoga Mat.* Inner Ocean Publishing, 2006.

Wood, Bliss. *Empowering Your Life with Yoga.* Alpha Books, 2004.

About the Author

Janice De Jesus is a freelance arts and features journalist. An avid yoga practitioner for 13 years, Janice is also a Certified Pilates Instructor and student yoga teacher.

She earned her MFA in Creative Writing at Mills College in Oakland, California and teaches ongoing creative writing classes in the San Francisco Bay Area. This is her first nonfiction book.

You can learn more about Janice at her web page at: http://janicedejesusauthor.blogspot.com or email her at janicedejesusauthor@gmail.com.

www.ingramcontent.com/pod-product-compliance
Lightning Source LLC
Chambersburg PA
CBHW030016290326
41934CB00005B/363